THE
POPE'S
ARMY

THE
POPE'S
ARMY

 500 Years of the
Papal Swiss Guard

ROBERT ROYAL

Herder & Herder
The Crossroad Publishing Company
New York

The Crossroad Publishing Company

Copyright © 2006 by Robert Royal

All rights reserved. No part of this book may be reproduced, stored in a retrieval system, or transmitted, in any form or by any means, electronic, mechanical, photocopying, recording, or otherwise, without the written permission of The Crossroad Publishing Company.

Printed in the United States of America
The text of this book is set in 10.5/13 Galliard.

Library of Congress Cataloging-in-Publication Data
Royal, Robert, 1949-
    The Pope's army : 500 years of the papal Swiss Guard / Robert Royal.
      p. cm.
    Includes bibliographical references and index.
    ISBN 0-8245-2395-4 (hardcover)
    1. Vatican City. Guardia svizzera pontificia – History. I. Title.
UA749.5.R69 2006
355.009456′34 – dc22
                                                            2005032734

ISBN 13: 978-0-8245-2058-8

1 2 3 4 5 6 7 8 9 10   10 09 08 07 06

Contents

Preface ix

1. Five Hundred Years of Fortitude 3
    A Modern Corps / 6
    The Long Papacy and the 2005 Conclave / 10
    The Modernized Conclave / 13
    Becoming a Swiss Guard / 18
    Legal Status in the Vatican / 20
    Die Vereidigung (Swearing-in Ceremony) / 24

2. "Defenders of the Church's Liberty": Pope Julius II and the Origins of the Guard 29
    A Weakened Papacy / 32
    Swiss Independence and Papal Independence / 35
    The Rise of Mercenaries / 38
    Julius Calls on the Swiss / 40
    The First Recruits / 44
    The Swiss and Papal Politics / 47

3. Consolidation and Trial: The Medici Popes, the Guard, and the Sack of Rome 50
    Years of Turmoil / 53
    Changes in Swiss Policies at Home and Abroad / 55
    Renewed Swiss Commitment to the Pope / 56
    Kaspar Röist's Reform of the Guard / 57
    Leo X's Death and Its Consequences / 59
    Pope Adrian VI and Early Reformation Politics / 61

    Clement VII and the First Threats to Rome / 63
    Charles V's Moves in Italy / 66
    The Colonna and the First Sack of Rome / 68
    Zurich's Recall of the Swiss / 71
    The 1527 Sack of Rome / 74

4. **Siege, Dissolution, Rebirth**   77

    A Renaissance Fortress and Palace / 79
    The Atmosphere during the Siege / 80
    The Spectacle of Benvenuto Cellini / 82
    Imperial Fury Unleashed / 83
    Damage to Charles V's Reputation / 86
    The Disbanding of the Swiss Guard / 87
    Silence about the Sack in Switzerland / 89
    Renewed Spirit in Switzerland / 92
    Commandant Jost von Meggen / 94
    Two Reforming Popes / 97
    Von Meggen as Diplomat / 99

5. **Years of Peace — and Napoleonic War**   101

    Kaspar Leo von Silenen's Command / 103
    The Talented Jost Segesser / 106
    The Swiss and the Battle of Lepanto / 108
    A Long, Uneventful Period / 112
    Years of Peace and the Altishofen Dynasty / 113
    The Popes, the Swiss Guard, and the French
       Revolution / 116
    Another Restoration / 120

6. **The Guard during the Unification of Italy and the Pope's Imprisonment in the Vatican**   122

    The Pope's Escape to Gaeta / 126
    Meyer and the Guard Prior to 1849 / 128
    Commandant Martin Pfyffer / 135

Meyer's Appointment to Command / 136
The End of the Papal States / 142
The Swiss and the "Prisoner of the Vatican" / 147
The Close of the Nineteenth Century / 151

7. **The Guard during the Two World Wars and the German Occupation of Rome**   154

World War I and Two Swiss Anniversaries / 157
The New Legal Situation / 159
The Swiss under the Concordat / 162
The German Occupation of Rome / 164
A Swiss Guard's Firsthand Account / 168
Kidnapping the Pope? / 171
The Final Assault and the Liberation of Rome / 172

8. **Modern Times**   175

Contemporary Threats / 180
An Unfortunate Interlude / 186
New Directions / 189

Epilogue   193

Notes   197

Index   203

Illustrations follow page 116

Preface

THIS BOOK is a popular account of the past and present of the oldest and, arguably, most distinguished military regiment still active in the world, the Papal Swiss Guard, or *Pontificia Helvetiorum Cohors* as they are known in official documents. The Swiss Guard is the smallest army on earth and serves the smallest nation, the Holy See (Vatican City State). Somehow its size seems to have had little to do over the centuries with its stature. How two very different human groupings — Switzerland and the seat of the Roman Catholic Church — came to form this singular entity will become clear in the following pages. The history of the Swiss Guard is tied not only to the emergence of Switzerland and Western Europe, but especially to the changing fortunes and developing roles of the modern papacy. At times, it is a story of great heroism and devotion, as well as of serious internal turmoil and external challenges that had to be surmounted in order for the Swiss Guard to survive for half a millennium in papal service.

There are already a few examples in print of what the Europeans call "scientific histories," scholarly volumes in German and French, that offer rather full studies of the Guard based on original documents in the papal and Swiss archives. Most of these are now old and accessible to only a very few people who can read those languages. They also tend to assume that readers will have a much greater command of continental European history since 1500 than is usually the case today. The present volume does not pretend to be a work of original scholarship and relies heavily in places on the professional historians. Yet as the Guard approached its five hundredth anniversary in 2006, it seemed right that it be known a little better by a much larger number of people for the work it has done and continues to do, over and beyond the colorful presence it provides for visitors to Rome and Vatican City. The present volume tries to convey a sense of what life for the Swiss Guard is like in Rome today, along with some of the drama of the Guard's history and the circumstances in which it came into existence and operates.

The idea for this book first emerged years ago in conversations with the Hon. Faith Whittlesey, formerly U.S. ambassador to Switzerland and currently chairman of the American Swiss Foundation in New York. We immediately thought it would be a good project, then somehow let it slip out of our grasp, only to take it up again when we received encouragement from many people on both sides of the Atlantic. I want to thank her and her assistant, Gene Waering, for their always professional support and encouragement. I am also grateful to Ambassador Raymond Loretan, Swiss consul in New York. In Switzerland, I received invaluable help from Amédée Grab, bishop of Chur; former Federal Councillor H.E. Flavio Cotti; Dr. Daniel Vasella; Alberto Togni; Dr. Joseph Jung; Dr. Christian Rey; and Roy Ryan. Early on in my research, Dr. Jürg Stüssi-Lauterburg, director of the Eidgenössisches Militärbibliothek, and Dr. Dominic M. Pedrazzini, a member of the library staff and specialist in several subjects including the Papal Swiss Guard, welcomed me in Bern and kept me supplied with crucial materials. Mr. Roland Buchs-Bins, former commandant of the Swiss Guard (twice, the only person ever asked to return after retiring), now at Fedpol in Bern, was very generous with his time and knowledge. In Rome, over the course of several trips, Major Peter Hasler, one of the long-serving Swiss officers, provided me with useful research references. Commandant Elmar T. Mäder patiently took me through the Guard's current operations and, even more importantly, gave me a sense of the spirit and ethos of the men who serve the pope today.

Stefan Meier, a former guard and now a photographer, provided many of the images here.

I am also grateful for the support of the Ulrico Hoepli Foundation, Zurich, Switzerland.

Closer to home, Dr. Dennis Bartlett, an experienced American military and security officer of wide historical and religious experience, did me the favor of reading the manuscript and catching several errors. Rachel Thurneysen-Lukow, a native-born Swiss and my next-door neighbor in the Washington suburbs, helped me to read and understand some sources written in Swiss dialects, a mystery to someone who merely knows German, like myself, and often, I am told, even to the Swiss.

This is an unusual story. When John Paul II died in 2005 and was succeeded by Benedict XVI after a brief papal conclave, the Swiss Guard received numerous applications, a few even from Protestants. The special role the Swiss play at such transitional times exerts a powerful attraction beyond what most people can express. I hope the following pages at least make a little clearer why the Swiss Guard still possesses some mysterious charisma and manages to communicate it to so many people even in the modern world.

THE POPE'S ARMY

Chapter One

Five Hundred Years of Fortitude

ON MAY 6, 1527, forty-two Swiss guards furnished protection for the fleeing Pope Clement VII. He rushed through the *Passetto,* a secret corridor along the top of the Vatican wall that ran then, as it does now, from St. Peter's Basilica down to the fortress along the Tiber River known as Castel Sant'Angelo. Today's Swiss guards still have the key to that clandestine escape route, which passes alongside and just above their quarters in the Vatican. Ironically, Clement was fleeing the troops of Charles V, the Most Catholic King of Spain and Holy Roman Emperor, who had invaded the papal city that morning and were beginning the massive pillaging of treasure and the slaughter of thousands that shocked all Europe at the time and is known to historians as the sack of Rome. The pope could see the carnage below from openings in the parapet. Cardinal Paolo Giovio shielded the pontiff from view with his own purple cloak as they ran together. The Swiss guards provided the military cover.

In a way, the Swiss who accompanied Clement into what would become a seven-month-long siege were lucky. One hundred and forty-seven of their colleagues died that day holding off attackers near the main altar of the old basilica, which stood on the same site as the present St. Peter's. Indeed, their commanding officer, Captain Kaspar Röist, was severely wounded during the fighting on the Vatican's walls and was carried back to his quarters —

only to be brutally murdered by the Spaniards as his wife, Elizabeth, watched. The forty-two guards who survived at first refused to retreat and agreed to go with Clement only when their substitute commander, Herkules Göldli, ordered them to carry out their sworn duty: guarding the person of the pope. In homage to these early displays of heroism, Swiss who become papal guards have taken their oath of allegiance each year on May 6.

On May 13, 1981, more than 450 years after the sack of Rome, when John Paul II was shot while passing through the crowds at St. Peter's by the Turkish gunman Mehmet Ali Agca, Swiss guards were still providing personal protection for the pope. The nature of modern threats is such that the guards now work closely with the Vatican's own police force, several intelligence organs of the Italian state, and the security agencies in the many countries that the pope visits. But the Swiss guards claim — indeed almost boast — that, wherever he goes, they always bear final responsibility for the safety of the Holy Father. Their fidelity to that responsibility, for a half millennium in 2006, gives them a certain right to make the claim. No other active military force has served as long. And despite their being unable to prevent the capture of the pope by superior forces at times during that long history, no pope has died at the hand of hostile forces on the Swiss guards' watch.

What kind of institution is this group of men known as the Swiss Guard? And what kinds of individuals are drawn to this service, which might seem an anachronism in the modern world? Most visitors to Rome probably think — if they think about it at all — that the Swiss guards exist just to provide a little local color for tourists around the Vatican. And that is partly true, at least in the sense that on formal or ceremonial occasions they have chosen to continue wearing uniforms whose design goes back near the time of their founding in 1506 under the "warrior" pope Julius II. Historical tradition has maintained that the great Michelangelo designed the uniforms, but there is no evidence either for or against this assertion. We know that a twentieth-century commandant of the guards studied Raphael's frescoes in the Vatican and restored the Swiss ceremonial uniforms to something resembling those depicted in the sixteenth century.[1] But who designed the uniforms Raphael drew remains unknown. Tourists and even the Swiss themselves have been known to refer affectionately to the uniforms as "clown suits." In any event, the Swiss continue the tradition simply because everyone seems to like it. The guards wear simpler all-blue uniforms and berets for more ordinary purposes such as controlling the flow of pedestrians and traffic at the Sant'Anna Gate. And the higher officers who do personal bodyguard duty with the pope during his travels wear the nondescript dark suits that seem to have become the standard uniform for personal security services around the globe.

So there is more to this story than history and pageantry. The Swiss Guard continues to represent a special combination of military virtues, idealism, and religious commitment that over centuries has made up the main motivation of the young men who are chosen, trained, and sworn into papal service. The requirements for applying to this small, but world famous, papal army are surprisingly few: a candidate needs to be a Catholic with a good reputation (*guter Leumund*) at home — as confirmed by letters from their pastor and local police chief; at least 1.74 meters tall (a little over 5 feet 9 inches) so as to be able to command authority at security checkpoints, and in good health. Some conditions, such as epilepsy, are disqualifying because guards spend long periods alone, often without the possibility of immediate medical help. Recruits must also be under thirty and have already completed basic military service in Switzerland, which is compulsory for all Swiss men (one benefit of this common background is that everyone is familiar with the same basic commands — in German — and with standard-issue Swiss Army weapons, which are now standard for the Swiss guards as well). Non-officers also have to be single. Historically, it has created both financial and moral problems when numbers of the entry-level guards are married;

even today, the Swiss have had to do fundraising in their homeland and the United States so that the children of the guards can be put into appropriate schools in Rome.

Finally, all Swiss guards have to be Swiss. This category, as might be expected, has become a little elastic in modern times. One recent guard was born Swiss but grew up in Ecuador when his family moved there for an extended period. Officers say that the essential thing is a certain "Swiss mentality," since the young men are packed into close quarters and do better when they all have certain similar habits and expectations. In 1992, the Swiss Guard swore in its first "non-white" member, Dhani Bachmann, who had been born in India and adopted by native Swiss parents in Hildisrieden in central Switzerland. Bachmann became intrigued with the idea of papal service, however, in the same way that most young men in Switzerland have over the centuries: he heard former Swiss guards in the area talking about it.

A Modern Corps

These modern recruits, like their more ancient counterparts, come to Rome for various reasons. Some are young and idealistic, others are looking for adventure, still others just need a break before they decide on universities or careers. While all guards know they are entering a corps that has a partly religious dimension, they come with different degrees of spiritual formation. Under current leadership, their spiritual lives are given a great deal of attention, as much as the physical and military exercises, study of the Italian language, and training in special security requirements. The guards have an official chaplain, do periodic religious exercises (usually when the pope is doing the same), but operate with a good deal of awareness about the varying ways of grace among modern twenty-year-olds. "We're all on a religious journey," says Elmar Mäder, the current commandant, "officers as well as the younger men."[2] Still, recruits must be active Catholics and are required to attend Sunday Mass.

It is not necessary to turn these men into choirboys to come to appreciate what they do and to see it as, in its way, something that the modern world does not have in great supply — a deep dedication and loyalty to duty adapted to the demands of our own age. The Swiss guards who helped Clement flee in the Renaissance were quite similar to the soldiers they fought against, though staunchly loyal to a different cause. The modern Swiss guards have a different set of responsibilities. Instead of outright warfare, they often have to combine security services with the tact and finesse of a diplomat. In recent years, they have become only too aware of how vulnerable all of the West's central institutions are to unprovoked attack, including the Vatican and the Holy Father. At the same time, they must carry out the vigilance and control necessary in a way suited to the pastoral mission of the modern popes. As will become clear in the following pages, the balance between these two very different functions is not always easy to achieve. But it must be achieved, for the precise reason that what the Swiss must do around the pope and Vatican City makes a real contribution to his ability to carry out his public ministry.

The Swiss guards operate under several constraints that other security forces do not. First, while they have all already done their required military service in Switzerland and have been trained to use the standard weapons of the Swiss Army before they are ever considered as candidates, recent popes beginning with Paul VI have ordered the guards not to carry firearms openly when they are protecting him at liturgies and public appearances. During those liturgies, the Swiss try to occupy positions best suited from a security standpoint, while the liturgical directors are always seeking to make them invisible in order to emphasize the religious nature of the events. With the papacy of John Paul II — a precedent that has already continued with Benedict XVI and is likely to be carried over into future papacies — the Holy Father has tried to come as close to the people as he possibly can, not only in Rome but in his travels around the world. "He believes he is protected by divine

Providence," said Commandant Mäder about John Paul II shortly before his death, "and so do we. But we also believe that we are part of that divine Providence."[3]

At the checkpoints to entering Vatican City, the Swiss guards do not display any weapons other than the halberd, the long spear with a special hooked metal head that was carried by the early members of the troop (the ordinary entry-level guard today stills bears the rank of "halberdier"). Officers admit that there are also more modern weapons at each post, which can be quickly deployed as needed. They deliberately refrain from talking in much detail, however, about exactly what those weapons might be, but guards are issued weapons such as the Swiss-made SIG 9mm pistol and train with other familiar firearms. After the attacks on the World Trade Center in New York and the Pentagon in Washington on September 11, 2001, the Swiss reevaluated the deployment of their forces in light of potential terrorist threats. Since 2002, guards have been able to take a course in martial arts, for example, and may receive specialized training at European academies for the types of security they perform. Whatever other adjustments may have quietly been made, there is no obvious physical difference at the main checkpoints. Italian police have established extensive, airport-level security, including metal detectors, for everyone who enters St. Peter's Basilica — and even the piazza in front of St. Peter's for special events. No such apparatuses have yet turned up at the four entrances manned by the Swiss: to the left of the basilica, the Holy Office Gate and the Arch of Bells (also known as "Carlo Magno," i.e., "Charlemagne" to the guards); to the right, the Bronze Doors (Portone di Bronzo) and the Sant'Anna Gate. The Swiss commanders, however, feel confident that they have sufficient security at the entrance to the Holy City using more subtle and largely invisible means.

Firm but diplomatic behavior is a constant necessity where the guards come in contact with the public. On the one hand, new recruits have to be trained from the moment of their arrival to begin to recognize as many as possible of the important religious and secular people who pass daily through the Vatican's gates — and accord them the respect many VIPs need. On the other hand, they have to challenge anyone unfamiliar who approaches, even those wearing clerical dress or looking important. They have to be able to size people up quickly. In years past, there have been several cases of people passing themselves off as bishops in order to penetrate the grounds of the Vatican. Fortunately, to date they have been harmless eccentrics. But on a couple of occasions, the guards have restrained belligerents and even had to use pepper spray. For most visitors to Rome, the guards will be the only official contact with the Vatican they will have: The guards know this and go out of their way to be polite and accessible as befits representatives of the Church, while exercising gentle control over curious visitors. And this too seems to have worked rather well and endeared the guards to people of many different backgrounds. Indeed, guards have married women from several different continents whom they met while on duty.

The Swiss guards provide many other security functions, most of them never seen by casual visitors, inside the Vatican as well. About 80 percent of their work consists in guarding the Apostolic Palace, the residence and workplace of the pope. For a force that numbers just over a hundred men, this takes long hours on duty, to say the least (sixty hours a week minimum on average and some night duty during which they sleep in beds stationed near security points). The further you penetrate in the palace toward the Holy Father the more Swiss checkpoints you must pass. Men are stationed at these points, as in the past, but more sophisticated electronic surveillance and magnetic ID cards are now part of the whole system. The hub for all activities is the Bronze Doors, which is situated just on the right-hand side of St. Peter's Square. There is always a sergeant of the Guard on duty and a sentry detail there when it is open; all guards going on duty report to that sergeant so that he can know where everyone is at any given time. Another sergeant in plain clothes roams through the Apostolic Palace, checking in with the various guards and making sure that all functions are being properly performed. The switchboard for the palace is also at the Bronze Doors so that all communications can be well coordinated, inside and out.

The Long Papacy and the 2005 Conclave

The length of John Paul II's papacy, more than twenty-five years beginning in 1978, brought many benefits to the Catholic Church and the world, but for the Holy See it has meant that there are few people still alive who know about certain essential procedures. For example, a papal conclave, the closed deliberations of the cardinals of the world who elect the next pope, had not been held in almost three decades prior to the election of Benedict XVI in 2005. The security challenges over those years have grown to be formidable. In the 1970s, electronic bugging devices, computers, and cell phones were either nonexistent or primitive by today's standards. In 2005, even casual readers of the press knew that security forces were taking steps to guard against such things as laser eavesdropping and other high-tech challenges. The Swiss guards, who are historically responsible for the safety of the cardinals and the secrecy of their discussions, had to rely on Vatican and Italian experts for that part of the job. But they continued to do all of the other tasks needed to assure the integrity of the papal election.

When John Paul II died in the Apostolic Palace on April 2, 2005, after long years of suffering from multiple maladies and of various speculations about the state of his health, it plunged the entire Holy See, the Swiss Guard among them, into largely unknown territory. For the Swiss, a papal funeral and a conclave are epoch-marking events. The guards are in a particularly good position to appreciate the kind of spirit that these moments can release. One Swiss guard, for example, who has done a dozen years of service in Rome, described the immediate effect of the announcement of John Paul II's death: "I don't know how many people were in St. Peter's Square that night — 60,000 or 80,000 is my guess — but I've had to handle all sorts of crowds there in all sorts of situations. I've never experienced anything like what happened. The minute the announcement was made, the whole group went absolutely silent. Not a peep anywhere. I don't know how long it lasted, but 80,000 people standing absolutely still in one place without anyone saying a single word: You felt something present that you are not aware of every day."[4]

John Paul II had taken great pains to spell out how the interregnum and the new election were to unfold, even at what point (after thirty votes), if necessary, the cardinals in the conclave should switch from a two-thirds to a simple majority. But it is one thing to lay out the general rules for such an event and quite another for those responsible for carrying it out in detail to decide how best to respect the wishes of the deceased pope. Long before, the commandant of the Guard had repeatedly talked with the camerlengo, Cardinal Eduardo Martínez Somalo, the Vatican official charged with running the Church during the *sede vacante* (empty throne) period, about what plans they should make. The camerlengo, who first announces to the world from the loggia of St. Peter's who has been chosen as the next pope, seems to have been in some uncertainty himself. He simply said that he did not want to prepare plans that might cause confusion if he later had to countermand orders. Swiss guards swear their obedience to the pope, who is their commander-in-chief, as well as to the cardinals who will run the Church in the period between one pope and another. Since neither of these authorities was prepared to decide on the details of the transition, the only thing for the Swiss to do was wait.

But Swiss being Swiss, they could not simply ignore things that had great potential for disorder. The commandant and his higher officers tried to prepare by studying the records that they possessed. These records were written by earlier Swiss guards and were therefore, of course, all in order, but were not nearly detailed enough. In the past, there had always been old-timers around who knew the ropes. As the plans for the funeral and new conclave developed, the Swiss compiled a thick file of protocols so that their successors will not face a similar vacuum. In the meantime, class after class of Swiss had come and gone, leading to a kind of tradition: outgoing guards on their way back to Switzerland would congratulate the new ones and predict that they would be the ones actually to serve in a papal election. The expectations went on a long time; when John Paul II died, more than fifty Swiss guards who had served under him returned for the funeral, and that was only a fraction of the hundreds of guards from the whole period. None of them, however, knew in much detail what the duties during a papal funeral and conclave might mean.

Some forms of duty were clear. From the time John Paul II died late on a Saturday until his body was laid in the tomb under the main altar at St. Peter's Basilica almost a week later, the guards posted a twenty-four-hour-a-day honor guard. The entire world saw the three or four million people who were eventually to file through the basilica, a line fifty persons wide and several miles long. People routinely waited eight to twelve hours for a few seconds' glimpse of the remains of the man some were already calling John Paul the Great. Crowds, particularly emotional crowds, are funny things, and, as the guards well know from dealing with them, funny things may happen. The universal experience of the guards on duty during those days, however, was not only that the crowds were orderly and reverent, but that they often went out of their way to thank the Swiss and others standing watch for the service they were rendering to a deeply loved leader. As could even be seen from television, the guards and other Vatican forces nonetheless took the security for the whole ceremony very seriously and did not slacken vigilance in the slightest. John Paul II's body was transferred from the Apostolic Palace to the basilica for the lying in state and the funeral with nearly the same level of protection he had gotten while he was alive. The Swiss provided an honor guard, of course, but officers in plain clothes functioned as a literal bodyguard right down to the moment the deceased pope was lowered into the ground. It was the final moment in their sworn service to him.

The Modernized Conclave

The sworn service continues, however, even when the leader changes, and the guards now took up their new duties toward the future pontiff. John Paul II's concerns for the Church and the cardinals continued after his burial. He had been part of two conclaves in 1978, both held in the Sistine Chapel, where the cardinals were then also housed. According to all reports, the conditions at the time were nothing less than primitive: spaces divided by hastily rigged ropes and blankets; awkwardness in getting help or medicines that might be needed; perhaps most embarrassing for a group of men with aged prostate glands, frequent trips during the night to distant toilets. John Paul II made sure that the cardinals would have basic comforts as they carried out their duties. He had a kind of hotel, the Casa di Santa Marta, built inside the Vatican to the left of the basilica. While this solved some personal difficulties for the electors, it provided a new security dimension. Cardinals are supposed to have no contact with the outside world when they are in conclave (in Latin, "conclave" means closed with a key). The cardinals had two choices about how to go back and forth between their residences and the Sistine Chapel: bus and foot. The Holy See's Security Corps watched them en route. The Swiss made sure they entered and exited safely. Such arrangements, however, obviously presented some new challenges if traditional prohibitions against outside contacts were to be protected, even though the cardinals remained within the bounds of Vatican City.

Since the death of the apostle Peter, traditionally considered the first pope and bishop of Rome, 262 other men have occupied his chair. It is the belief in this direct succession that gives the pope his ultimate authority as bishop of Rome and temporal head of the Roman Catholic Church. So keeping the process free of improper outside pressure and threats to the cardinal electors has been one of the significant duties, since its creation, for the Swiss Guard. In the sixteenth century, when the guards first performed this task, the main threat to the process was simple bribery. Powerful families in Rome and the various royal courts of Europe have been known to treat the papacy as just one more powerful office for which to compete, and intrigued for it accordingly. Some of those squabbles led to no small problems for the Church and for the papacy. In modern times, the pope in Rome can exert vast influence over many parts of the world, even those that are not Catholic — witness John Paul II's role in the breakdown of Communism in Eastern Europe. So worldwide attention was focused on the Vatican in 2005 for serious secular as well as religious reasons. To judge from news reports following the 2005 conclave, despite the attention, not much of what happened within the walls of the Sistine Chapel during the conclave leaked out.

So-called "spies" have long been a part of the papal entourage, just as there have been agents of various types who have infiltrated the highest offices of all the major world powers. There is good reason to believe that, in addition to the use of agents, electronic eavesdropping on the Vatican has been going on since at least the 1950s. In the tense decades of the Cold War, not only the Communist countries but also Britain, the United States, and Italy itself had an urgent need to know what the Vatican's stance would be toward all kinds of modern political developments. Support for an atheistic system that persecuted and martyred Christians by the tens of thousands was not a natural inclination for the Holy See, but it was still important for the West, as well as the East, to know what moves the Vatican might be considering. Particularly in Italy, where a strong and militant Communist party nearly came to power in the years after World War II, the stakes for the United States and the non-Communist segments of the Italian government were high. Stories that there were "collaborating" priests or bishops who reported to the Polish Communists in John Paul II's days are common. But it is clear that at least since the election of John XXIII in 1958, and probably even during the papacy of his predecessor Pius XII, serious surveillance of the Vatican was already under way, even by friendly governments.

Worries about bugging and clandestine influence on the conclaves in the Sistine Chapel emerged around the same time. The Swiss guards are primarily a personal bodyguard for the pope, and while they have modern weapons and specialized technical equipment to carry out that task, they do not have the super-high-tech means required to stop modern electronic surveillance. It has been quite possible for a while now to record conversations inside a room by focusing a laser beam on a window. That kind of snooping and many others well known to the intelligence community were warded off as much as possible during the 2005 conclave by cooperation and sharing of information by various Vatican, Italian, and international services, including the Swiss. But the traditional Swiss role comes into play after all the technology has been put into place and the conclave must begin, as it has throughout the centuries, with the electors gathering together and being sealed into the Sistine Chapel for their deliberations.

The process is well known and continues basically unaltered except for a few details. By the time the cardinals arrived to vote, all access had been essentially cut off except for the entrance to the chapel from the Cortile San Damaso. (This courtyard is the same one in which the new guards are sworn in every year.) All those involved in the conclave, from the cardinals and their aides, to the cooks and cleaning men and women, were solemnly sworn to secrecy. Surprisingly, whether by an error or because it is believed they are already so sworn by the nature of their papal service, the Swiss guards were not asked in 2005 to take the common oath, though they were present as it was being done. They were on watch at all entrances and exits throughout the conclave and sometimes, at need, within the sealed area. But once everything had been fully prepared for the formal voting, the camerlengo shouted out the traditional order *"Extra omnes!"* ("Everybody out!") and within minutes they were all gone. At that point, the lowest-ranking cardinal, which means the one most recently added to the hierarchy, closed the door from the inside and locked it.

Outside, the doors were closed with metal seals by a delegation that included a representative of the Holy See's Governatorato (the formal government within the city), a delegate/technician from the Vatican Museum (since metal seals are going to be applied to some very old and valuable doors), and, in his role as final guarantor of the safety and integrity of the proceedings, the commandant of the Swiss Guard. Unlike in the past, since the cardinals no longer remain in conclave within the Sistine Chapel until they select a new pope, this procedure had to be repeated and the necessary security measures rechecked each time the cardinals left and returned. Fortunately, the conclave of 2005, like most recent conclaves, lasted only a short time, which simplified the logistics and security considerably. The election of Cardinal Joseph Ratzinger as Pope Benedict XVI came on only the second full day of the conclave. By ancient custom, once the cardinal had received the necessary number of votes, three things happened: the candidate was asked if he accepted; having accepted, he was asked what name he wished to be known by; and then he went briefly into a small room that opens in the wall near the bottom left of Michelangelo's *Last Judgment,* the so-called *sala di pianto* (roughly, "room of tears") to put on temporary papal vestments already prepared in three approximate sizes — small, medium, and large — in anticipation of all eventualities. The new pontiff then emerged and received a vow of loyalty from each of the cardinals who had elected him.

Shortly after that, he exited from the secure area of the Sistine Chapel. One of the very first people outside to meet and congratulate him was the commandant of the Swiss Guard, who was waiting in the *sala regia* with an honor guard of eight men. But in the first hour or so there was neither time nor place for full formalities. The camerlengo quickly went to the loggia, the balcony that looks out over St. Peter's Square, and made the ancient declaration *habemus papam* (we have a pope), specifying his name.

The commandant of the Swiss Guard went with him. Since the camerlengo is not an interim pope and at that point there was already another pope, it is difficult not to speculate that perhaps the traditional role of the Swiss commander in the formal announcement was to make sure that the name announced to the world was in fact the name selected by the cardinals. Because of the speed with which these events now move in today's media age, the commandant was alerted by means of his radio earpiece, just as the announcement was made, that the new pope had started to come over to the loggia as well. Popes do not travel without Swiss guards, even across the one hundred yards or so from the Sistine Chapel to the loggia, and on such occasions the highest authorities must be present. So the commandant had to run back to escort him to his first public appearance in front of the world as Benedict XVI.

One humorous curiosity about the 2005 conclave was that the cardinal elected was living, like all the other cardinals, in the new Casa di Santa Marta. The papal apartments once occupied by John Paul II had been sealed, and there was no staff to take care of anyone, let alone a pope, in the Apostolic Palace. So Benedict XVI was escorted by the Swiss back to his temporary quarters in the Casa di Santa Marta. At the dinner the pope gave for the cardinals and other dignitaries that evening, he and the Vatican secretary of state, Cardinal Angelo Sodano, called over the Swiss commandant and asked him whether the pope should move from the simple room, which he had been assigned by lot, as had all the others. The pope's preference was to keep it simple, especially when he was offered the "patriarchal" suite: "Oh, no, I could never be compared with a patriarch," Benedict XVI replied, forgetting, it appears, that he was now pope, a much higher post than a patriarch. The Swiss assured him that they would set up security for him wherever he wished, even in his small room, but within a few days the sheer volume of business he had to conduct convinced Benedict that he had to take larger quarters after all. The Swiss moved along with him.

A curious endnote to the transition: Cardinal Ratzinger, the future Benedict XVI, had long lived right across the street from the barracks of the Swiss Guard. They often used to joke that they could look right into one another's windows. The guards were only too happy to provide service in the Casa di Santa Marta, but, of course, they prefer it when the pope is safely inside the Apostolic Palace where the routines are established and the chances for mishaps diminished. A characteristic of the two most recent popes is the sheer physical austerity of their lives within the papal apartments. Karol Wojtyla (John Paul II), as is well known, lived very simply, and the rooms in his time were sparse to the point of being barren. Joseph Ratzinger (Benedict XVI), a theologian, lived just as simply, with one exception. As a highly learned and intellectually curious man, he had accumulated a considerable library. It not only had to be transferred to the papal apartment; it had to be moved and re-created in the exact order in which it existed, since, like many intellectuals, the new pope has a highly personal cataloguing system. All that further complicated the pope's entry into his usual quarters and the return to normal procedures for the Swiss.

Becoming a Swiss Guard

A papal funeral and a conclave are among the most solemn occasions for the young men of the Swiss Guard. Many new recruits doubtless enlist for their initial two-year stint after imagining themselves at those events as well as performing daily service in close proximity to the pope. Young guards will often speak, without prompting, of having been fascinated back home when they heard stories of Swiss swearing to defend the Holy Father, with their own lives if necessary. (Perhaps that is why, following the death of John Paul II and the election of Benedict XVI, about a hundred young men — a number that even included some Protestants and is almost equal to the entire active Swiss force — applied to the Guard.) Applicants may be interviewed in Neuhausen am

Rhine, a small town north of Zurich near the highest waterfall in Europe, where the Guard has a recruiting office. After their application and interviews, the candidates who are selected are ready for their trip to Italy. In earlier days, new recruits were usually hardy young men from rural areas or soldiers already used to life in the field. They made the trip from Switzerland over the Alps down to Rome on foot (the first guards in 1506 even did it in winter). Today, their modern successors typically arrive in groups by train three times a year. The new recruits start at the bottom of the pecking order, not only in military rank but in living arrangements. Housing is tight in the Swiss Guard barracks, so many at first find themselves in the ten-bed dormitory that the guards call "California." With seniority, the guards may pass on to double or single rooms as they become available. The food in the canteen is basic Swiss fare, until recently even cooked by Swiss nuns, the Sisters of Divine Providence from Baldegg, Switzerland. The tailoring of uniforms, for some reason, is the one day-to-day function that has traditionally remained in Italian hands.

The new guards immediately start formation in two main areas, one more or less practical, the other more theoretical. They learn practical military affairs such as specific Swiss Guard traditions (including proper uniforms, behavior in the various Vatican settings, and other peculiarities of papal service); they drill in the courtyards and the gardens of the Vatican — individually and in groups — with the halberds they use during actual sentry duty, under the eye of an officer with the nickname "Sergeant Barbetta." They become familiar with the handling of other arms, take periodic target practice at a nearby Italian police range, care for equipment, do regular physical training in a gym located in the barracks, and study martial arts, primarily for self-defense. On the more theoretical side, they all pass through a recruit school that instructs them about the nature of the Vatican and its personnel; they begin to acquaint themselves with Rome and Italy; and they take intensive Italian language courses in the library attached to the barracks (most guards leave after two years with certificates stating they have reached proficiency equivalent to the first or second levels of European university study). Increasingly, guards also study English because it is the most useful language in dealing with people who approach them. As soon as they have mastered the basics, the new recruits are ready for simple sentry duty. Deeper entry into the ways of the Swiss guards, however, usually comes with experience and interaction with the older members of the corps.

The younger men typically say that the training is not as hard as they undergo in the Swiss Army, but parts of the service are more difficult than they may seem. Everyone likes seeing the guards in full-dress uniforms on special occasions, for example. Few people realize, however, that wearing ancient military garb consumes a great deal of energy. Most of the young guards come to realize this the first time they have to wear the metal helmet (which weighs about nine pounds) and ceremonial armor (which may weigh as much as fifty pounds) for several hours in the hot Italian sun. Even young people in good physical condition feel severe fatigue after carrying around an added fifty-nine pounds for considerable lengths of time. The new guards also train to be able to remain motionless carrying this weight during sentry or honor-guard duty. The officers claim they have even perfected psychological techniques to make an itch go away.

Legal Status in the Vatican

The new recruits who come to Rome today operate under a structure that was put in place by Pope Paul VI. Paul VI is often thought of as a slightly regressive pope who came on the heels of the liberalizing John XXIII. Both characterizations are highly misleading. It was Paul VI, for example, who set in motion the process of modernizing the Vatican's security forces in line with his overall desire to do away with traditional monarchical trappings of the papacy, which, he believed, no longer reflected the role of the pope in the modern world. For him, papal pretensions to any vestige of temporal power were over. The pope henceforth would be a pastor, not a ruler. Relations with the democratic government of Italy after World War II were good: the government recognized and appreciated the role that Pius XII had played in preventing the destruction of Rome and in resisting the Germans. Unlike France and Germany after their democratic transitions, in Italy whatever government anticlericalism existed did not threaten the Church's spiritual mission. Relations between the two sides were cordial, and the pope sought to keep them that way. And one of the concrete ways in which he showed his trust and goodwill was by sweeping reform of the Vatican security forces.

In 1970, the pope directed Cardinal Jean Villot, then Vatican secretary of state, to eliminate or to restructure virtually all of the existing papal security forces, with the sole exception of the Swiss Guard. He explained in a letter how "our Military Corps, even though much esteemed and existing until now in the service of the Holy See, no longer correspond to the needs for which they had been created."[5] There were several groups included in these military corps. Some, such as the Honor Guard of His Holiness, had existed for almost as long as the Swiss, though they were of a much more "honorary" than military character. Early on, they were known as Knights and Broken Lances and then were reorganized in the 1800s as Noble Guards. As late as 1963, potential members had to be able to show that they came from families belonging to the Italian nobility (such as it was after Italy became a democracy after World War II) for at least a century, and their commander was selected by the pope from the vague but numerous cohort of Roman princes and dukes. This sort of body, which was now to be transformed into an informal club of a kind, clearly belonged to an age of papal temporal pretensions and of the ongoing conflicts between the Vatican and a unified Italy.

The pope's modernization cut even deeper, however. Another military corps, the Palatine Guards, had been created in 1851 by combining the old Milizia Urbana del Popolo di Roma (Urban

Militia of the Roman people) and the Guardia Civile Scelta (Select civil guard). It had performed very valuable service during World War II in protecting Vatican possessions from the occupying Nazi armies (its numbers had swelled to over two thousand men for that purpose). It was also disbanded. Its sentry duties were assumed by the Swiss, and the larger protection of the Vatican passed to the traditional Gendarmeria Pontificia (Pontifical police), which itself was disbanded in 1971 and reconstituted as the Corpo di Vigilanza dello Stato Vaticano (Security corps of the Vatican State). The Corpo di Vigilanza continues to have general security responsibilities for visitors and access to the Vatican gardens, as well for the safety of the Vatican train station, helicopter port, museums, and other sites. It also handles basic policing and legal matters inside the Holy City.[6]

Though the Swiss Guard was the only body among the Pontifical Armed Forces that was not affected by Paul VI's reforms in 1970, it currently operates under a set of regulations that were adopted in 1976. Throughout its history, the Guard as a body has signed formal agreements with the Holy See, not least because the Swiss government has usually wanted certain assurances about the type of military service its citizens would be performing for what is, in reality, a very small foreign power. The often repeated description of the Guard as "the world's smallest army in the world's smallest state" is true. But even so small a military corps works better when its structure and operations are carefully spelled out. Troubles have arisen historically within the Swiss Guard in periods when its regulations were out of date and no longer corresponded to contemporary conditions. Paul VI's sweeping reforms in the 1970s did not radically alter existing arrangements with the Swiss, partly because the Swiss had not undergone radical changes in duties during the century between 1870 and 1970, when the papacy was slowly moving toward its current form.

The 1976 regulations reconfirmed that the pope is directly in charge of the Swiss Guard. By contrast, the Corpo di Vigilanza is run by the Vatican's civil government, the Governatorato. As direct dependents of the pope (or the College of Cardinals in the interim periods between the death of one pope and the election of another), the Guard's commander is chosen by the Holy Father. The command structure can be somewhat confusing because the whole corps has dual rankings. For instance, though only the size of a company (in 2005, 110 men), the Swiss Guard as a body was accorded the rank of a regiment by Pope Pius IX in 1852. The main officers individually also have dual ranks. In 2005, Colonel Elmar Theodor Mäder served as commandant (*Oberst*). Under him are a vice commandant, Lieutenant Colonel Jean Daniel Pitteloud; a chaplain, Mons. Alois Jehle (an officer in the Swiss Army and an honorary lieutenant colonel in the Guard); three second lieutenants of varying ranks (Major Peter Hasler, Captain Frowin Bachmann, Captain Pino Coco); and a sergeant major (*Feldweibel*), Christoph Graf. One traditional feature that was not eliminated by the 1976 regulations: the commandant, vice commandant, and major are lay members of the papal household and Gentlemen of His Holiness, two honorary rankings.[7]

The corps is divided into three squadrons (*Geschwadern*), two primarily German-speaking and one primarily French-speaking, which reflect the demographics of Switzerland: roughly 70 percent German, 20 percent French, 10 percent Italian, and 2 percent Romansch. In theory, the three squadrons allow for a regular work rotation: two days on duty, one off. But it is the very nature of the papacy that almost every week brings special events and high-ranking dignitaries. The Swiss Guard has established different protocols to welcome kings, presidents, prime ministers, and other high-ranking officials at state visits, and guardsmen are not exempt from duty if some special demand happens to fall on the third day of their rotation. Since all the guards already put in long hours on their regular duty days, the added burden of special events can lead to sixteen-hour shifts and long periods without sleep, especially when guards come off a night-duty rotation and have to turn immediately to a special service. At least thirty guards, sometimes more, are also present at the pope's Wednesday general audience. In addition, some in street clothes mix with the crowd while others watch from rooftops with binoculars or keep open evacuation routes. Seventeen Swiss go with the pope to his summer residence in Castel Gandolfo just outside of Rome. Needless to say, all these irregular hours are draining, and they make it difficult to organize recreational and cultural programs that are both good in themselves and help keep up morale. The Swiss soccer team, Guardia FC, has won the championship in the Vatican league in recent years, but, as in other sports, it typically has to forfeit several games every season because of work schedules. Current recruiting levels have kept the corps at a manageable but tight force of 110, but officers believe that just ten more men, if they could be recruited and supported financially, might allow them to form four squadrons and rotate them in a manner that would take considerable pressure off the halberdiers.

Die Vereidigung (Swearing-in Ceremony)

Every guard probably remembers the day of his swearing-in as the high point of his life in the Swiss Guard. The day of the swearing-in ceremony is one of many contrasts in a city like Rome. It typically begins on the morning of May 6 with a Mass celebrated by the pope and a laying of a wreath in commemoration of the guards who died on that date defending Clement VII from the invasion by imperial troops in 1527. Then the pope receives the officers, the new men, and their families in a special private audience, usually in the Sala Clementina. The new recruits for the whole preceding year are there, all those who have entered into the papal service since the preceding May. This means that many of the guards being sworn in have already spent the better part of a year in Rome, mostly in sentry duty and controlling visitors.

The difficulties this kind of crowd control raises at the Vatican are quite evident on the day of the swearing-in itself. Few people realize it, but the Italian state today takes care of the security check for people entering St. Peter's Basilica. In appearance, it is nothing more than passing through airport-style security: an X-ray machine for bags and a metal detector. In practice, it is a mess, particularly on those special days when there is something happening inside the Vatican, including the swearing-in, because to enter the Cortile San Damaso, a large and elegant courtyard between the Sistine Chapel and the Apostolic Palace, where the swearing-in takes place, you have to pass through the general security for St. Peter's. Italians are notorious for their inability to form orderly lines, and they do not acquire new virtues when they are visiting the Vatican. It is quite a sight to see the swarms of Italians and foreign visitors mixed together with the rather stunned Swiss parents and friends of the guards, who clearly never expected anything like the mob scene of which they are a part. The swarm trickles through the security check at a maddeningly slow pace for anyone used to other ways of dealing with crowds, but by Italian standards it is relatively efficient because at least it moves.

Past the security check lies a different world, a world at least partly Swiss in its order and precision. Guests for the ceremony show their invitations and go briskly through a Swiss checkpoint outside the Portone di Bronzo, the large bronze doors to the right of the basilica where visitors to the pope and the Apostolic Palace typically enter. On the day of the swearing-in, the Swiss direct the visitors up the marble stairs to the courtyard. As each person enters the open space, ushers appointed by the Swiss quickly identify which kind of invitation that person possesses and escort people to their seats if they are VIPs or direct them to the other sections reserved for parents and friends. The VIP section is something to behold. Not only is there the usual array of cardinals and high Vatican dignitaries, but there is significant representation from the Italian government and the foreign diplomatic corps. Perhaps most impressive, however, are the military officers decked out in full-dress uniforms of every imaginable color, from Italy and Switzerland to Canada and the Philippines, and sporting medals in shameless quantities. The Swiss commandant and the higher officers themselves are in full sixteenth-century array, which means they wear traditional uniforms with white ruff collars, breastplates, and dress helmets with white plume (the commandant) or red (all the rest of the officers and the enlisted men). In spite of an air of festivity and expectation, the more than three thousand people typically assembled for the ceremony show a quiet order and calm.

At 5:00 p.m., precisely the designated hour, a clock in the courtyard chimes. Two doors open on a balcony that juts out from the back wall of the Sistine Chapel. Four trumpeters emerge and blow a brief fanfare. They reenter immediately, and the doors close. A sharp verbal command comes from a tunnel on the opposite side of the courtyard underneath the Apostolic Palace. A muffled sound of marching can be heard that becomes more and more distinct. The Swiss Guard band marches out in silence with its instruments, followed by the new recruits carrying their halberds, typically twenty-five to thirty in recent years. This little platoon make no other sound than the slight clink of their breastplates (about half of their armor is at least three hundred years old) as they march and swing their arms in unison. In that setting and given that these are real guards of a real ruler, it is hard not to imagine yourself back in the sixteenth century. Of course, in a way it is merely a ceremony, but in this case a ceremony involving a solemn pledge of loyalty and a willingness to die in defense of the pope that has been taken by Swiss recruits for half a millennium. And everyone present cannot help but feel the accumulated weight of that tradition.

When the band and recruits have lined up at attention in two rows under the Sistine balcony, the staff sergeant presents them to the pope's representative and to the commandant. The latter walks to a podium and pronounces a brief exhortation to the men in the three main languages of Switzerland: Italian, French, and German. He urges them to live up to the tradition that they are about to inherit, to keep themselves mentally and physically fit, and to acquit themselves like the guards of the past both in their formal duties and in the way they live their private life, including its spiritual dimension. A clerical representative of the Holy See then takes the podium and in four languages (this time including Romansch) makes a similar plea and reads the actual words the guards will pronounce, each one in his own mother tongue, when he swears allegiance. Each guard is then called by name by the sergeant. He answers "present" and knocks the butt of the halberd on the pavement before handing it to the man next to him (there are stories, perhaps some of them even true, of unfortunate cases in the past where nervous new recruits have slammed the halberd down onto the foot of the man standing alongside). Each man then marches halfway around the perimeter of the courtyard before advancing to the center. There a small group of men holds the banner of the Guard. When ordered, the new recruit takes the flag in his left hand, raises his right hand with three fingers extended in homage to the Holy Trinity, then shouts out in a loud voice:

> I swear I will faithfully, loyally, and honorably serve the Supreme Pontiff, Benedict XVI, and his legitimate successors, and also devote myself to them with all my strength, sacrificing my life to defend them if necessary. I take on these same duties with regard to the Sacred College of Cardinals whenever the See is vacant. Furthermore, I promise to the Captain Commander and to my other superiors respect, fidelity, and obedience. This I swear! May God and our Holy Patrons assist me!

It takes no more than fifteen or twenty minutes for all the new men to be rotated through this ceremony, after which the crowd gives them a standing ovation.

At this point, it is the time for the band to go into action. A small but accomplished ensemble, they begin with traditional Vatican and Swiss anthems and hymns but are not beyond taking chances. In 2005, they ventured out on "I Will Survive," a pop tune surprisingly well orchestrated for this kind of ensemble. There is some of the usual oompah music and display of complicated drumming skills — just enough music to top off a festive occasion. After this brief display, the men are dismissed by the commandant. They form ranks and march the perimeter of the courtyard and then out through an archway underneath the Vatican Museum.

It is difficult to imagine what they must be feeling at that point, especially since the route back toward the barracks takes them through cavernous tunnels broken by courtyards from which there are breathtaking vistas of the whole of the Vatican, beautiful buildings interspersed with the peculiarly lush green of the Holy City's well-kept gardens — a brief march but a setting that, even to an outsider, seems almost like a dream. The barracks are, by contrast, rather modest next to the Sant'Anna Gate on the Vatican's outskirts. But for Swiss twenty-year-olds, many of whom have never been outside their native cantons, to return to barracks through that environment after such an event and to spend a few years in close proximity to the Holy Father must — at least sometimes — feel like living at the edge of Paradise.

Chapter Two

"Defenders of the Church's Liberty"

Pope Julius II and the Origins of the Guard

THE YEAR 1506 was marked by several special events, special even for so rich a cultural period as the Italian Renaissance. It was in the spring of that year that Pope Julius II laid the cornerstone for the magnificent new basilica of St. Peter, whose basic design had been created by the well-known artist Donato Bramante (Michelangelo and other famous artistic figures would revise or add to the design in the century and a half that it would take to complete the new structure). The new church was meant to replace the crumbling older basilica whose origins, on the traditional site of the apostle Peter's martyrdom, went back over a thousand years. The ambitious project also reflected the pope's vision of restored prestige for the entire Roman Catholic Church. In the same year that the new church was begun, Julius planned and executed a military campaign to retake lands lost from the Papal States (the wide swath of territory across the middle of Italy ruled by the popes) in recent decades, including their second most important city after Rome, Bologna. Michelangelo was commissioned soon after the city fell to cast a huge equestrian statue in bronze of the "warrior pope." And with Julius as he approached Bologna and entered the city was the special corps of soldiers he had recruited from Switzerland and received in Rome in January of 1506, the Papal Swiss Guard.

The Swiss were a logical choice for this service. From the end of the thirteenth century until well into the eighteenth century, they were regarded as among the bravest and most reliable of fighting men in all of Europe. Just fifteen years before Julius created his papal guards, King Louis XI of France had decided that he too needed a special bodyguard and selected one hundred Swiss, who officially became his Garde de Cent Suisses.[1] For hundreds of years after, armies in several European nations imitated Swiss tactics and training and also vigorously sought to recruit Swiss mercenaries, as we shall see, so much so that the Swiss government had to take care that its own men fighting abroad would not become a threat to their own country — or to one another if they ended up fighting on opposing sides in foreign wars. To possess an elite group of Swiss bodyguards in that age was the rough equivalent of having at your disposal a highly skilled modern secret service or even a special forces unit such as the U.S. Delta Force or Navy Seals.

But why would a pope need such warriors?

A modern reader may think that the kinds of political, military, and artistic ambitions pursued by Julius II have little to do with, and may actually have hindered, the authentic spiritual mission of the papacy as that mission has been redefined in the past few centuries. Many people in the early sixteenth century did not see things that way. Church and State were not separated in modern fashion within countries. And the Church as an international actor seemed to almost everyone to need real independence to resist the perpetual threat of worldly powers. The Swiss Guard, along with other papal forces, afforded the pope one way to assure his own independence. At the time, those who supported a papacy that also had real political powers were not wholly wrong — especially given the difficult circumstances of sixteenth-century Europe.

Anyone who visits Rome today for the first time will probably be surprised at the massive and steep walls that still surround much of the small Vatican City State. We do not usually think of churches or religious property as requiring special protection from secular powers, particularly in modern democracies such as Italy. All the formalities and obstacles to immediate access, including the Swiss guards stationed at key entrances, may thus appear to be mere holdovers from a bygone era. It has not always been the case — indeed, throughout history it has typically been quite the opposite — that secular movements and authorities are willing to restrain themselves vis-à-vis the Church. As recently as the 1930s and 1940s, for instance, the Catholic Church faced serious and simultaneous threats from Communist governments in several parts of the world, most notably in Stalin's Soviet Union, from the Nazi regime under Adolf Hitler in Germany and its offshoots in several nations, and in Italy itself from the Fascist government of Benito Mussolini. It helps us to understand what Julius II and many other Church leaders in his day had in mind, as different as it may be from our own conceptions, if we remember that just sixty years ago Rome itself was controlled by Fascists — and soon after by a Nazi occupation force. Both of these secular movements systematically tried to intimidate the Church. Toward the end of World War II, the Germans even developed plans to kidnap the pope, take him to Germany, and hold him hostage as U.S. forces and the armies of the other allies closed in on their homeland.

As one commentator rightly (if a little floridly) observed in 1930, at the height of the several threatening political movements:

> Those who perform the task of watching over the revered person of the Supreme Pontiff and of participating in the great ceremonies of Vatican City so as to assure their exterior order, represent their Swiss Homeland, of which they guarantee the nobility and fidelity. At the same time, they confront the new Italy [i.e., Fascism] as symbolic and visible witnesses to the spiritual independence that is one of the

necessary conditions of the very organization and ministry of the Church.²

Of course, the guards could not have withstood an assault by massive Nazi or Fascist forces, though there were precedents of small numbers of Swiss holding out against, or even defeating, much more numerous adversaries, as we shall see. In any event, their mere presence interposed a not unimportant and clearly visible line between State and Church even in the twentieth century.

This relatively recent period may still look like ancient history for some people today, but the Church has lived through various abrupt political changes as well as the rise and fall of whole civilizations. And it does not forget that what has happened once can return again with a vengeance. So it is not mere flattery or sentimentality to say that the Swiss guards have deserved the traditional title *Defensores ecclesiae libertatis* (Defenders of the Church's liberty). They did so quite literally from 1506 until the present, and first got the title from Pope Julius II, the "warrior pope," who created them and appreciated their help in the wars among Italian cities and foreign powers, which were a conspicuous feature of European history throughout his papacy.

A Weakened Papacy

In 1506, there were many exterior military and political threats to the papacy, but there were equally formidable challenges within the Church as well. Julius had been elected pope a few years earlier (1503) at a difficult time for the Church. Almost two centuries of turmoil had weakened it considerably and dispersed its spiritual authority. For roughly the middle half of the fourteenth century, the papacy had been in exile at Avignon in France under the "protection" of the French king in what was known as the "Babylonian Captivity." In 1378, splits in the College of Cardinals led to two popes being elected by rival factions: Urban VI and Clement VII. To resolve the dispute, a council convened at Pisa in 1409, but succeeded only in failing to depose the two claimants while establishing a third. It was eventually at the Council of Constance in 1419 that matters were settled by the election of Martin V — though rival claimants lingered on in obscurity even for about a decade after that. The damage that this century of claims and counterclaims did to the prestige and authority of the papacy as an institution, and even to its spiritual mission, was deep and pervasive.

One additional threat to the papacy was the decree at the Council of Constance (1414–18) that regular councils should meet — which gave rise to what historians have called the conciliar movement. The Western Church had never been governed through councils of bishops, and it is not surprising that differing and contentious interpretations of the authority of pope and council followed for the next half century and more. The movement failed but remained a constant threat to the popes, especially when secular powers allied with one or more cardinals wanted to restrict or even to eliminate papal independence for worldly reasons. Several popes in the sixteenth century, including Julius, faced real or planned councils that sought to depose them, often because of the ambitions of secular rulers. This meant that, for nearly two centuries after the achievements of the High Middle Ages, Europe had lived with a weak, compromised, or even divided spiritual authority, which was constantly beset by internal religious problems as well as international power politics.

And if this were not enough, the troubles of the papacy had led to immense turmoil in the large area of central Italy over which the popes had governed for hundreds of years. Accustomed as we are to separation of Church and State, the very notion of a spiritual leader who also rules over a secular territory seems, on its face, illegitimate. The more astute among the medieval philosophers and lawyers were aware of such difficulties too. The pope did not as a rule claim temporal authority over all of Christendom. Various kinds of secular rulers had their own proper functions and authority. In the circumstances of the day, however, it was difficult to see how the papacy could be independent — in its spiritual and administrative dimensions — if it was dependent, politically and economically, on the competing powers within the European continent. That perspective is not ours today, but for a Renaissance pope it appeared necessary to his Christian office that he possess lands and adequate resources for his needs. So the "warrior pope" Julius II was, by the lights of his time, not undertaking something shameful in trying to reconquer and pacify the traditional Papal States. He was seeking to restore the dignity and independence that had been crumbling for almost two hundred years.

The problem lay not only with the institution of the papacy. Europe's emerging nation states quarreled bitterly with one another — so much so that when several popes in the late fifteenth century called upon them to unite and defeat the very real Ottoman Turkish threat in the eastern Mediterranean (the Turks had finally captured Constantinople in 1453), they continued to play off European and Turkish influences in pursuit of their own relative advantages within the European power system. The Turkish incursions would come to an end only with their defeat at the very gates of Vienna in the seventeenth century, almost a century and a half after the papal appeals. It is hardly a surprise that a Europe divided and intriguing against itself to this extent with danger staring it squarely in the face could only be intermittently relied upon to support a weak temporal ruler who also happened to be the spiritual leader of Christendom.

It is important to realize that quite serious threats to the papacy as a spiritual entity came from the Christian secular powers as well. The Emperor Maximilian, for example, got it into his head during Julius's papacy that it might be wise to unite papacy and empire in his own person. This is not as quixotic as it may seem today. Most political regimes throughout human history have had some substantial relationship with the spiritual leadership within their borders. Even in nations with which we are rather familiar, such things have happened. When Henry VIII, who in his early life was a staunch defender of Catholicism, felt himself frustrated in his attempt to divorce and remarry, he not only rejected papal authority but proclaimed himself head of the Church in England. The very nature of political and spiritual powers, which necessarily involve some authority over human lives, constantly threatens similar confusions.

Swiss Independence and Papal Independence

Why did Pope Julius turn to the Swiss when he could not rely on other European powers to protect the prerogatives of the Church and Christendom itself? Primarily it was because the Swiss had for many years been an invincible and thoroughly reliable fighting force. To begin with, Swiss tactics were unbeatable, so much so that King Ferdinand of Spain, best known for his support with Queen Isabella for Columbus's expeditions in the New World, boasted that he had begun to form a Spanish force of "armed men ordered in the Swiss fashion."[3] Machiavelli, a cynical but shrewd observer, reflected in his *Art of War* that there were political, moral, and military reasons why the Swiss had grown so skilled: "The superiority of the Swiss is a result of their ancient institutions and the lack of cavalry."[4] In this common view of Switzerland, its traditional liberties and the absence of the usual mounted knights had forced the Swiss to become fierce fighters, especially by comparison with the rather cautious and gentlemanly chivalry typical of Italy and other European states. Machiavelli admired these Swiss so much that, on the basis of their relentless and seemingly unstoppable military prowess, which had been known to defeat armies twenty times the size of their own numbers, he even dubbed them the "New Romans." In his judgment and that of his contemporary Francesco Guicciardini, the Swiss had achieved things militarily for which there was no comparable precedent in ancient Greece or Rome.

There had been Swiss in the service of the popes prior to 1506, though historians dispute exactly what to call them, since they were not exactly the same as the personal bodyguards to the Holy

Father that have existed, with some breaks, down to the present day. Records exist of Swiss serving the pope as early as the middle of the fourteenth century, during the so-called "Babylonian Captivity" when the papacy had been captured and moved to the city of Avignon in southern France. A century later there is much other evidence of popes from Sixtus IV to Alexander VI concluding alliances with the Swiss and sometimes making use of Swiss soldiers of different kinds, especially to ward off the threats to Italy from the king of France. (In a historical irony, Swiss mercenaries also fought for France and helped it become united and powerful.) Later popes would set up substantial garrisons in places they controlled, such as Avignon, Bologna, Ravenna, and Urbino. In spite of these varied precursors and successors, the Papal Swiss Guard, properly speaking, appears only in the early 1500s.

The Guard, like the other Swiss troops that the pope was to employ, were part of the larger number of the Swiss mercenary units that dominated European warfare in the fifteenth century and beyond.[5] Few people realize the extent of these fighting forces. There were approximately one million Swiss employed as fighting men outside of Switzerland between the late fifteenth and early nineteenth centuries. Scholars estimate that the Swiss were the "main nerve" and made up approximately one-fifth of the French Army from the times of the Italian wars in the early sixteenth century to the French Revolution. There was a special Swiss attachment to the French king. Pierre de Brantôme could already say in the sixteenth century, "When we have a body of Swiss in our armies, we believe ourselves invincible."

The Swiss did not do mercenary service in France alone. They also served in the armies of Holland, Spain, Austria, Sweden, Naples, Savoy, and Britain. Some four thousand Swiss fighters were involved in the American Revolutionary War. A little later (August 10, 1792), six hundred Swiss soldiers were massacred by revolutionary forces while they were defending the French monarch Louis XVI at the Tuileries Gardens. (After 1792 Swiss units were disbanded in France, and after 1848 mercenaries became illegal under the Swiss constitution.) The Swiss government tried for a long time to put a stop to this mercenary service — which was driven mostly by the need of poor mountain dwellers, who had multiplied because of growing prosperity, to better their condition by fighting abroad — but most of the time it had to settle for controlling the terms of service contracts.

One reason the mercenaries had to be controlled, especially by the fledgling Swiss confederation, was that their military prowess was so great that it might ultimately result in dangers to Switzerland itself or its national interests. So the Swiss government carefully spelled out regulations for what it called *Reislauf,* or mercenary services. Foreign governments that wished to recruit Swiss fighters had to obtain permission from the Swiss state, which treated the available military manpower as a kind of state monopoly, even going so far as to issue authorizations for certain numbers of soldiers and export licenses in the same way that they might control grain, salt, or other commercial transactions.[6] Yet the individual cantons remained technically the masters of the mercenaries; in addition, the hired troops were commanded in their own language by Swiss officers, fought under their own flags, and were disciplined on the basis of their own regulations by Swiss judges. In theory, the Swiss cantons could recall them at need, since even abroad the Swiss fighters were subject to the laws of their own homelands.

The Swiss forces had developed a distinctive mode of fighting during the formation of the Swiss confederation as an independent European entity. Men carrying long pikes and the halberd (the weapon the Swiss guards still display at several places in the Vatican even today) were formed into tight phalanxes, the first infantry forces in Europe able to resist cavalry since the armies of ancient Rome. These well-disciplined units were virtually unbeatable from 1470 to 1515. The introduction of gunpowder, which was used in artillery pieces and in the arquebus, changed the military dynamics, notably at the 1515 Battle of Marignano, where the Swiss suffered a crushing defeat. After that defeat, the Swiss Army, which earlier had looked as if it might turn Switzerland into a continental European power, never fought outside of the country again.

To this day, Switzerland is highly organized for defense: all Swiss men do compulsory military service. But the Swiss Army's extensive and impressive network presents virtually no offensive threat.[7] In spite of changed circumstances, the Swiss infantry were still the best in Europe, and that is why France made them an integral part of its forces. Swiss fighting men were still highly sought after because of the fierceness and skill they had developed in guarding their own independence. Swiss independence arose largely because of the practical demands of geography. The many valley communities isolated by complex mountain ranges were generally left to run their own affairs. While the structures that emerged were usually oligarchic at the local level (as were many of the ancient Greek and medieval Italian city-states), at the regional, national, and international levels the Swiss were used to making their own decisions and defending their own collective way of life. Individual defensive skills were further honed, even among young boys, by the need to respond to threats to flocks from wild animals such as wolves or bears — and from aggressive neighbors. The internal cantons of Uri, Schwyz, and Unterwalden in particular emerged as a loose federation called the *Waldstätte* (Forest Cantons).

The Rise of Mercenaries

As Swiss prosperity increased in the thirteenth century, mostly because of the pasturing of horses and cattle and a subsequent increase in dairy products, larger economic structures became advantageous to the valley dwellers and city dwellers alike. And the opening up of the Gotthard Pass to increased traffic meant greater facility in conducting trade between the Low Countries and Italy. This wealth and commercial activity, however, attracted the attention of the Austrian Habsburgs, who, in the late thirteenth century, wished to control intercourse between the two halves of the Holy Roman Empire. This would lead to further struggles by the Swiss for independence over several centuries. Paradoxically, the threat from the emperor stimulated greater resistance. When the Holy Roman Emperor Rudolph took over the key city of Lucerne in 1291 and blockaded the members of the Forest Cantons, the three regions in that confederation signed a mutual defense pact on August 1 of the same year. The pact involved only a small portion of what today is regarded as Switzerland, but historians typically point to 1291 as the beginning of the Confederatio Helvetica or *die Eidgenossenschaft,* as it is called in German.

This seemingly modest grouping of largely rural peoples proved itself capable of remarkable military feats. In 1315, for example, when the Habsburgs tried an assault on Schwyz, the Swiss showed they could be as shrewd as they were fierce. They lured the emperor's troops into a narrow valley near Morgarten and then sprung a trap. The mounted knights in heavy armor were unable to maneuver in the cramped circumstances. The Swiss defenders first threw stones and other heavy objects down on them from the hillsides. Then they attacked with axes and halberds (the halberd then, as now, has a hook that enable infantry to pull mounted knights down off their horses). When the battle was over, the Habsburgs had lost two thousand men and the Swiss only a dozen. All over Europe, Morgarten was talked about as something new and unexpected. Over the next decade, the Swiss confederates formed even closer alliances with one another and with the major Swiss cities, and the empire granted them freedom from serfdom.

The freedom of the cities depended on their military discipline and skills with weapons. The Swiss knew how to attack effectively with what they had. Weapons were typically two-handed. The pike and halberd were long and heavy, but were wielded skillfully (Swiss pikes were imitated everywhere in Europe until muskets and bayonets became widely available in the eighteenth century). Infantry often carried a six- or seven-foot sword. Typically, they wore light or no armor, which might slow down movement. The Swiss forces relied more on ability to maneuver and well-coordinated units for defensive purposes. Crossbows — an early weapon that could be used at a distance — were common and effective, since they were in widespread use in hunting at home. (The early legends of William Tell and other Swiss figures probably combine authentic historical elements with largely mythical ones, but they capture the spirit of independence and cooperation that emerged in what would become Switzerland.) All of these features made Swiss soldiers something new among the medieval military forces.

Julius Calls on the Swiss

So it was only natural that Pope Julius II turned to the Swiss when he began to plan out how to restore the fortunes of the Church in Italy and throughout Europe. As we have seen, he was a military man himself. That was only one side, however, of his extraordinarily energetic personality. Though his hair was already completely white by the time of his election at the age of sixty on October 31, 1503, he gave no impression of being old. As the great historian of the papacy Ludwig Pastor describes him:

> Always active, always moving, with a devouring activity, constantly running vast projects around in his head, extremely opinionated and violent, he often drove people who had business with him to despair.... Physically and morally, he had the nature of a giant; everything in him, passionate desire, vast conceptions, went beyond common measure... and if he inspired fear, it was never mixed with hatred; for there was not to be discovered in him either pettiness or a vile egotism.[8]

Popes of the period often behaved very much like secular rulers in the ways they sought to secure their interests: marriage alliances between secular members of the family and nobility in various Italian cities; financial arrangements that secured the goodwill of potential rivals; and for good and bad — and notoriously — by the appointment of papal "nephews" (*nipoti*) to the College of Cardinals to assure that the family's interests were watched over even there. Julius got his start in ecclesial politics by this route. His uncle Pope Sixtus IV (Francesco della Rovere) was by all accounts a truly spiritual man and an accomplished theologian who on the basis of his own talents had earned the leadership of the Franciscans. Furthermore, his personal behavior seems to have been, unlike that of other Renaissance popes, quite proper. But as pope, and the (true) uncle of Giuliano della Rovere, Sixtus knew it was wise to appoint him cardinal while he was still a young man. Unlike many such appointments, this one brought a man of real energy and talent into the upper echelons of the Church. As a modern biographer rightly says of Giuliano's accomplishments during the thirty years he was a cardinal: "He was a major figure in the politics of Italy long before he became Pope Julius II."[9]

The future pope was not a great diplomat, nor was his private life exactly everything a cleric's should be. Still, he had several virtues. For instance, though he was given many lucrative benefices, he did not spend the proceeds on lavish living, as did many in similar circumstances. For the most part, he used his wealth as a patron of the arts and in the construction of several palaces and fortresses. His character seemed to have been straightforward and friendly, a trait that earned him friends even amid the complex intrigues of Renaissance Europe. Giuliano generally disobeyed doctors' orders, which — given the awful state of medicine in the period — may be one reason why he was so robust and energetic compared with most of his contemporaries. And his military and political campaigns as pope were not undertaken solely for personal gain. He sought, within the understanding of his time, to stabilize the Papal States, which had long been in turmoil. For that task he was willing to use or block foreign powers, as seemed expedient at any given time, especially since he faced a formidable Italian foe in the city of Venice. It seems clear that he would have preferred — other things being equal — to expel the influence of all foreign "barbarians," France in particular, in order to free Italy from foreign domination and to heal internal division, something that would not happen until the middle of the nineteenth century.

Simply put, Julius II's central project was to restore the honor of the papacy partly by making it a powerful temporal monarchy, the political master of Europe, but especially of Italy. We are not accustomed to thinking of religious figures as secular leaders, but the situation of the Church by the fifteenth century needed desperate reforms both within and without. And the Renaissance was a period when the nation states that we take for granted were just emerging. Spain had become united under Ferdinand and Isabella just over a decade earlier. France was still groping toward unity. The great historian of the Renaissance Jacob Burckhardt, who understood many dimensions of the period that are no longer familiar to us, appreciated Julius II and even went so far as to say that "in all essential respects he was the saviour of the papacy."[10]

Julius energetically established good government and order in papal territories, bringing back safety to Rome's often dangerous streets. He also had to tackle the reform of papal finances, police, and other offices. The beautiful Renaissance city that was already starting to emerge got an additional boost from his tireless promotion of the arts, especially painting, sculpture, and architecture. It was Julius who gathered together some of the recently discovered classical statuary in the Belvedere courtyard of the Vatican (including the Laocöon, discovered in that epoch-making year 1506), which provided the nucleus of what is today the Vatican Museum. Julius is probably most remembered today for the alleged clashes he had with the equally difficult Michelangelo over the time it was taking to complete the frescoes in the Sistine Chapel.[11] But it should not be forgotten that Julius had the good sense to hire the great artist and let him carry out his conceptions without interference.

Because of the demands of his day, he was necessarily a military leader in addition to everything else. In the absence of secular rulers who could run central Italy, the papacy had become by default a city-state of its own. Popes took on some of the characteristics of secular princes and, in Julius II, even became warriors. Julius was so intrepid in his military expeditions, which were mostly aimed at eliminating foreign domination over the Italian peninsula, that he was known as *il terribile* (in Italian, not "terrible" but "awe-inspiring"). As one of his biographers describes his vision: "For him, the dignity and authority of the Church were inextricably associated with the temporal power of the papacy, and throughout his pontificate, he saw his primary task in the defence of papal territory and the consolidation of papal control over the temporal government of that territory."[12]

Soon after his election as pope in 1503, he realized that he needed a corps of personal bodyguards who would be both loyal and tough. His mind turned naturally to the Swiss for several reasons. First, Julius had seen with his own eyes the terrible skill of the Swiss in wars in his home region near Genoa. As cardinal, he had petitioned the king of France for Swiss troops to pacify the area: "He claimed [in 1495] that if he were given 2,000 Swiss infantry, he could deliver the whole of the 'Rivier di Ponente,' the coast to the west of Genoa, including Savona."[13] The troops were not forthcoming, however, and the king of France turned his attentions elsewhere. When they finally did attempt the campaign, it turned out quite badly, though it instilled some fear of Giuliano among the Italian princes. The area between France and Italy was his place of birth, and "his contacts and influence there constituted one of the reasons why he was considered to be so dangerous to the peace of Italy."[14]

The impetuous cardinal had better evidence of Swiss abilities when he went with the French king Charles VII to Naples in 1491, where he witnessed from close-up how well the Swiss could fight. Nothing that happened over the more than ten years before his election in 1503 changed that opinion. As we have seen, many Swiss had become soldiers in the service of various European powers because poverty in their home regions left them few alternatives. Mercenaries are generally not very good fighters — and with good reason. Who really wants to fight and possibly die for money and a cause that usually does not involve any deep personal commitment? Yet the Swiss had a reputation throughout Europe of being a kind of "moving wall," which is to say a human barrier to attack that could not be easily broken. As in any army, the quality of individual soldiers and units could vary quite a bit. Overall, though, the Swiss were exceptional fighters.

Another factor in Julius's decision was what might be called, even then, Swiss neutrality. Obviously, Switzerland was not as nonaligned in principle in the sixteenth century as it is today. At the same time, it did not fall naturally or by choice into steady alliances with the major European nations at the time: Spain (and later the Holy Roman Empire in Spanish royal hands), France, England, or the main Italian powers such as Florence, Venice, Milan, or even Rome. Switzerland was a democratic confederation. Julius could not count on any automatic loyalty of history or interests, but he could — and did — believe that he could create a select body of men to whom he could entrust his personal safety. As the history of the past five hundred years demonstrates, he was right, not only for himself but for all his successors.

The First Recruits

He relied on one Swiss adviser in particular to bring the plan to fruition: Peter von Hertenstein, a cleric who had made a name for himself by performing various tasks for popes since Innocent VIII. In the latter part of 1505, Julius called him to Rome and explained what he needed. Von Hertenstein in turn suggested Kaspar von Silenen, a distant relative with a strong reputation as a military man, to become the first commander of the Swiss Guard, an idea that Julius II accepted. (In later years, since the commandant was a member of the papal household, the post was much sought after, not least because the patrician families that normally sent men to fill it had an unparalleled diplomatic observation post.) Von Hertenstein went back to Switzerland with a letter from Julius asking for two hundred men. The famous Fugger banking family provided the funds for recruiting and transporting the men selected to Rome. But several obstacles arose.

The Swiss government was again trying to control the number of citizens who got involved with foreign princes on military expeditions. And there was renewed opposition in Switzerland to the whole idea of mercenaries, not least because two sets of Swiss, one fighting for Ludovico il Moro of Milan and the other for the king of France, had just faced one another in 1500, which might have resulted in much fraternal bloodshed. The Swiss Diet tried to prohibit recruitment. Individual cantons, however, found the habit hard to break. Exceptions were allowed for certain kinds of duty, especially in France, and the papal recruiters suddenly found themselves in competition for men with the allure of French money, luxuries, and the possibility of booty. By contrast, papal service mostly involved sober guard duty, even though the person being guarded was the Holy Father. Von Hertenstein pointed out that the force of two hundred was a personal and palace guard, not an offensive army. Yet the climate of opinion had its effect: the prelate was able to sign up only 150 instead of the 200 men to march south to Rome.

They set out right away in the depth of winter and, as Julius requested, took the short route over the Gotthard Pass on dangerous roads. In spite of conditions, they all arrived safely. On January 22, 1506, like most travelers from the north down to the time of modern air travel, they entered Rome through the Porta del Popolo. Smartly clad in special uniforms, they marched to Campo de' Fiori, still one of the central piazzas of secular Rome, and then to the Vatican itself, where they took up residence. Almost exactly six months from the time he had left Rome, the ever remarkable von Hertenstein, despite all difficulties, had recruited and returned to Rome with Julius's personal guards.[15]

But times were unsettled, and Julius wanted to settle them quickly. After some feints and false starts, he moved boldly in

1506 to retake Bologna for the Papal States with three thousand Swiss soldiers and his Swiss Guard. This campaign was so successful that it evoked astonishment from no less a figure than Machiavelli. In a famous passage in his *Discourses* entitled "Very Rarely Do Men Know How to Be Altogether Wicked or Altogether Good," Machiavelli reproaches Giovampagnolo Baglioni, the tyrant of the city of Perugia, because when Julius stopped in his city on the way to Bologna, "carried along by that fury with which he governed all things, he put himself with a single guard in the hands of his enemies." The tyrant, says Machiavelli, was foolish because he did not "crush his enemy at a stroke and enrich himself with booty, since with the pope were the cardinals with all their delights."[16]

For once, however, Machiavelli was wrong about self-interested motives. Julius had been escorted into the city by the Swiss Guard, and other commanders and had taken the precaution of making sure that Perugia's army was moved outside the city before entering. Modern historians have uncovered evidence that trying to take Julius under these circumstances would have been very dangerous indeed.[17] Julius was nobody's fool, and if he entered Perugia with the Swiss Guard as his primary protection, it was because he knew they were sufficient for his purposes. Perugia in 1506 may be the first place in which it is possible to discern the difference the Swiss Guard made in the conduct of the papacy — in those days a direct military role.

Julius was not finished, however, with making use of the Swiss to bolster the Church against various threats. In 1509, he joined the League of Cambrai in defeating Venice, but no sooner had that occurred than Julius realized that France itself now presented the most immediate threat to the temporal interests of the papacy. And so emerged a policy that would be followed sporadically by him and his successors as conditions allowed: Italy, divided into many competing city-states, had to be drawn into some sort of unity or at least alliance with Rome and at the same time studiously keep out foreign powers. It was a difficult balancing act, especially since the various cities were constantly appealing to one or another foreign power to help in disputes with local rivals. No one could have played this game perfectly, but Julius II played it very well. By these and other means, his temporal prestige and that of the papacy as a whole rose considerably, even sometimes if at the immediate expense of the spiritual mission.

The Swiss and Papal Politics

At the same time, Switzerland was being petitioned by various nations for Swiss troops. The pope needed more himself but was not able to work out an alliance. In fact, he was informed that Switzerland needed all its men for its own purposes. Matthew Schiner, bishop of Sion, enters here as one of the great Swiss statesmen of all time, sent to convince the Diets of Switzerland and of the empire to support the pope's policies. An eloquent humanist and correspondent with Erasmus, Schiner had been on missions for the pope to lands as widely divergent as England and Venice. King Francis I of France is said to have remarked that "the cardinal's eloquence has caused me more concern and danger than all the pikes of the Swiss."[18] Burckhardt called him *vir inter exactae virtutis imperatores potius quam inter senatores numerandus* (a man to be numbered among the rulers, of clear excellence, rather than among mere ambassadors). Schiner skillfully presented the current situation as one of emperor and Swiss alike protecting the spiritual sword of the pope — obviously a very high service. It did not hurt his case that what they would protect the pope from was the rival temporal power to both, France.

In 1510, Schiner's work bore fruit. An alliance agreement allowed Julius to recruit six thousand Swiss mercenaries and use them any way he wished except against other Swiss. In return for proper financial considerations, the Swiss agreed not to form alliances or allow recruiting by other parties opposed to the pope; the pope promised to take the Swiss side and provide other benefits to the several cantons in all international negotiations. But fate interrupted these clear arrangements. A failed expedition at Chiasso soon after, in which the Swiss had to return home, brought blame on Schiner. And when the pope, in discussions with the Swiss at Bologna, failed to pay up money owed, the Swiss felt as if they had been treated as a subject nation rather than an equal and independent ally in a diplomatic partnership. The cantons sympathetic to France, furthermore, pushed for a break with Rome. The central Swiss cantons, always less inclined toward France, prevented that from happening. But a split had opened up more sharply in Switzerland itself.

And on top of everything, Julius II — for all his gifts and energy — now seemed fated to fail. He expected that, deprived of allies, Rome would be attacked and he himself deposed. Perhaps owing to stress, he fell ill several times with a fever. But failure was not in Providence's plan for Julius. Indeed, the first thing he did when he recovered was to bring together various nations, initially Rome, Spain, and Venice, into the Holy League for the protection of the pope and the Church, which was formally announced at Santa Maria del Popolo in Rome on October 5, 1511. Somehow he even succeeded in presenting this political alliance as a religious duty, a frequent papal claim that secular rulers of the time knew quite well how to ignore. Huldrych Zwingli, one of the prominent Swiss leaders during the Protestant Reformation, had no great love for the Church in Rome, but he understood why Swiss troops were setting off at one point to fight for Rome: "They saw the sad state of the Church of God, of the Mother of Christianity, and they regarded it as evil and dangerous that every tyrant could attack with impunity, and to satisfy his own rapacity, the common Mother of all Christians."[19]

Julius's forces, bolstered by the Swiss, were victorious at Pavia in 1512, fighting with a zest and enterprise worthy of him. They even took Milan, partly sacking and despoiling it. On July 5, 1512, Pope Julius II officially proclaimed the Swiss "Defenders of the Liberty of the Church." They were given two banners. One bore the papal keys and the arms of the Papal States with the inscription: *Dominus mihi adiutor; non timebo quid faciat mihi homo* (The Lord is my helper; I will not fear what man may do to me). The other banner had the pope's family (della Rovere) arms. Schiner designed a silk flag for each canton. This was a high point for the Swiss in the service of the pope. A Venetian historian wrote of them at the time: *Helvetii ceteros perterrentes quales leones inter lupos* (The Swiss are exceedingly frightening to many, like lions among wolves).

Perhaps one way to arrive at a just appraisal of what Julius and his Swiss collaborators achieved is to look at contemporary reactions. When Julius died, there was an unprecedented outpouring of public praise for him in Rome, a city of inveterate factions, even by some enemies, because, as one put it: "This pope rescued all of us, all Italy and all Christendom, from the hands of the barbarians and the French."[20] (Julius's unfinished tomb by Michelangelo in Rome's St. Peter in Chains, the titular church of Giuliano della Rovere from the time he was made a cardinal, includes the sculptor's famous statue of Moses, who saved his own people from powers who threatened their freedom and religion.) Julius did so — or at least others thought he had succeeded in his efforts — by his own personal energy and the clever use of those around him, such as the Swiss, of whom he had need. The Florentine politician and historian Francesco Guicciardini offered more ambiguous praise in judging that Julius neglected important spiritual dimensions of his office: "Certainly worthy of great glory, if he had been a secular prince."[21] The astute Jacob Burckhardt saw in him a mix of greatness and concern for something other than his own glory that spontaneously attracted praise: "Julius found poets to eulogize him, because he himself was no mean subject for poetry, but he does not seem to have troubled himself much about them."[22] The warrior pope died during the night of February 20 or 21, 1513. On his deathbed he did not fail to remember the Swiss Guard: *Ipsi servabunt nobis et Ecclesiae Romanae fidem prout hactenus fecerunt* — "They serve us and the Roman Church and down to this very moment they have kept faith with us."

Chapter Three

Consolidation and Trial
*The Medici Popes, the Guard,
and the Sack of Rome*

THE FORTUNES of the Swiss Guard, always closely connected with the fortunes of the pope, took a sharp turn with the successors of Julius II. Except for a brief interlude (1522–23) when a Dutchman presided over the Church as Pope Adrian VI, from 1513 to the fateful year of 1527, the prominent Medici family of Florence controlled the papacy in the persons of Leo X (Giovanni de' Medici) and Clement VII (Giulio de' Medici). These two men were quite different in outlook and abilities from Julius — and from one another. Neither had Julius's determination to protect the Church militarily; both were more interested in the kind of political, cultural, and religious projects more familiar to them from Florence. To a certain extent, these might be viewed as closer to our modern notion of what a pope should be and do, particularly in the case of Clement VII. But their combined efforts would lead to disastrous consequences for the city of Rome, which was sacked in 1527, and to deadly developments for the Swiss guards, who would lose their first two commanders in battle, as well as fight and die in large numbers defending the pope from invaders.

The Swiss played a major role in the long series of events leading up to that somber conclusion. Swiss cardinal Matthew Schiner of Sion, whom we have already met as one of the architects of Julius II's alliance with Switzerland and of the creation of the

Swiss Guard, was instrumental in getting Giovanni de' Medici, son of the legendary Lorenzo il Magnifico, elected pope in 1513 with the name Leo X. The new pope was believed to be a strong opponent of France in Italy and a supporter of the interests of the newly freed Italian city of Milan. Leo was almost the polar opposite of Julius: where Julius had been forceful and unrelenting, Leo was peaceful and easygoing. Furthermore, perhaps because of his Florentine background, Leo felt more comfortable in the presence of humanist scholars and artists than of soldiers and courtiers. The day after his election he proclaimed that he intended to make peace among Christians, who were shedding too much of each other's blood. He even asked the Swiss to help in this peace movement. Count Carpi, the Holy Roman Emperor's representative in Rome, reported back to the imperial court that the Medici pope "will be more a gentle lamb than a lion."[1] In the abstract, all these seem like good qualities in a pope, but as we shall see, those virtues could, in the turbulent circumstances of Renaissance Italy, sometimes turn into vulnerabilities, if not vices.

In the immediate aftermath of his election, Leo X put on a spectacle to impress the Romans — and perhaps to help transfer their allegiance from the late lamented Julius II to himself. On the feast of his namesake, St. Leo, he held a magnificent procession from the Vatican to the Church of St. John Lateran, the bishop of Rome's official church. This was officially called the *sacro possesso*, the pope's official "taking possession" of his episcopal seat. But nothing like Leo's procession, observers said, had been seen in Rome since the time of the ancient Roman Empire. The way was strewn with laurel and ilex leaves, and houses displayed brocades and draperies from their windows. The procession itself consisted of brightly clad cardinals and other high-ranking Church officials; standard bearers and mounted captains from Rome's several districts (*rioni*); Roman noblemen and their households, including members of the prominent Orsini and Colonna families; Florentines and representatives from the other Italian city-states; and many other colorful figures.[2] The Swiss guards in full papal livery — in this instance in blue, red, and gold, the colors of the Medici coat of arms[3] — surrounded the pope as he moved along the route under a silk canopy (*baldacchino*) carried by eight Roman patricians. He sat on a white Arabian horse that he had previously ridden at the battle of Ravenna.

In several public discourses shortly after this triumphal demonstration in Rome, Leo lavishly praised the Swiss but stated that he did not intend to employ Swiss mercenaries in the Italian wars. He intended to retain the highly prized Swiss Guard only for his personal use. When political conflicts arose at this early stage in his papacy, he preferred helping threatened Italian cities such as Milan with direct money subsidies instead of military assistance. And to the credit of his fiscal honesty, if not to the benefit of the Vatican treasury, he paid off the debts to the Swiss cantons for soldiers hired by his predecessor, Julius II. But there was a negative side to all this papal peacemaking and largesse. Pope Leo was very good at spending, so good in fact that it was later bitterly recalled that he spent not only the considerable sum that he inherited in the papal treasury from Julius II, but his own and his successor's revenues as well.

Leo, like all the Medici, was skilled in diplomacy and in hiding his ambitions under the guise of patriotic projects. The Medicis had a natural weakness for ideas of a consolidated Italian power in central Italy and even, as Machiavelli recommended in *The Prince*, of Medici domination of the whole of Italy. Early reactions to his election anticipated that he would sharply depart from the bellicose attempts to "free Italy from the barbarians" by his predecessor, Julius II. But circumstances as well as natural inclinations soon forced him into quite different paths. Before long, he too would be sending Swiss troops north to protect papal and Italian interests. In addition, Leo was the originator of a highly dangerous game of pitting French against Spanish, and vice versa, as threats loomed within Italy. These shifts in alliance could be of considerable use in the short run, but in the long run they accustomed foreign powers to using armed forces on Italian soil. It became all but inevitable that one of them would think the solution to all problems would be control of the entire peninsula. This was the origin of the eventual disaster and the slaughter of the Swiss that was to occur in Rome under Clement VII.

Years of Turmoil

To understand how all that happened we have to look more closely at the development of foreign incursions into Italy. Shortly after Leo's election, the French under King Louis XII captured Milan. The papacy could not tolerate French control of an important city like Milan, which would probably lead to further encroachments on papal power. Fortunately, the Swiss moved in and defeated the French, retaking the city. This was such an amazing exploit that Machiavelli — no easy man to impress — and the Venetian envoy Paolo Giovio thought it greater than anything they had read about in Greek and Roman antiquity. Leo sent Cardinal Pietro Bembo, an eminent humanist and orator, to thank the Swiss and ask them to help in his general policy of peace throughout Christendom. But their view came to be that the way to make peace was by force of arms, and so to convince Louis XII of France to leave Milan alone and to recognize territories the Swiss had gained in what is today called the Ticino. This was a hard task, since the king of France's interests lay in controlling Milan, and several other powers — the Swiss, the Venetians, and Rome — could not allow him to exploit that city without feeling threatened themselves.

To complicate matters, because of a temporary convergence of interests, Leo and Louis XII decided to make peace with one another. No sooner had that happened than Leo found out that Spain and France were plotting to put together an alliance of some kind. Louis's daughter Renée was to be married to one of King Ferdinand's sons, and the dowry was supposed to include Milan, Genoa, and Naples. Spain, which already controlled the area around Naples and much of southern Italy, would thus represent a possible second threat to the whole peninsula, this time from the south. Leo calculated that the French had approached the Spaniards because of the threat of the Swiss and had resolved to lessen that threat in order to make the new alliance unnecessary. As it turned out, this political marriage did not take place, and Leo wound up allying himself with the Swiss themselves. But with the death of Louis XII and the coronation of his successor Francis I on New Year's Day 1515 the stage was set for a new war.

The main battle in that war definitively changed the Swiss military stance. Various Italian states formed an alliance to resist the French forces and engaged them near Marignano in September of 1515. The Swiss forces in the coalition held out bravely, but owing to last-minute help to the French by Venice, their positions were overrun. (The Romans and Swiss alike resented this treachery on the part of Venice, and the Venetian ambassador in Rome did not dare to show his face in public for many days, once the news reached the city.) At Marignano about twelve thousand men, mostly Swiss, perished. Francis I wrote a letter to his mother saying, "For two thousand years no one has seen so fierce and cruel a battle." He was so proud of his unheard-of victory against a Swiss army that he had a medal made with the inscription *Primus domitor Helvetiorum* (First to dominate the Swiss) and another *Vici ab uno Caesare victos* (I defeated those whom only a Caesar could have defeated).[4] Naturally, all this struck fear into the heart of Leo. There seemed no way to protect the papacy now from a French invasion.

But the French king was worried about provoking a new alliance of England, the Holy Roman Empire, and the Swiss against him if he pushed his success too far. The pope and the king decided to meet in Bologna on October 3 to sign a treaty. Leo passed first through his native Florence; a fresco by Giorgio Vasari in Florence's Palazzo Vecchio commemorates his return and prominently features the Swiss guards, who traveled with Leo to the Bologna meeting. In the negotiations, the pope and the French king arrived at a temporary arrangement. More importantly, they set the stage for the concordat between the Vatican and France, which was signed the following year and essentially governed Church-State relations in France until the French Revolution in 1789.[5]

Changes in Swiss Policies at Home and Abroad

Leo's policy of trying to make peace left the Swiss cardinal Schiner on the sidelines, but other factors now arose that led to a crisis among the Swiss. First, the defeat at Marignano — a virtually unprecedented shaking of Swiss confidence in their armed men — forced a reassessment of how to act in the complexities of European politics. And at this very moment, the Reformation also struck Switzerland, dividing the country before it had really had a chance to grow into a full nation, as the other European powers were beginning to do. Most historians, whatever their point of view, believe that this kept the cantons that made up Switzerland from pursuing any united action for the next two centuries. Given these divisions, those seeking peace had the upper hand, and toward the end of 1516 France and Switzerland were to sign a treaty of "perpetual peace," which gave the French Milan and the Swiss territories they had conquered over the previous fifteen years and also spelled out arrangements that would lead to certain mutual economic benefits.

Ironically, the Swiss now became a major source of infantry for France. Francis I alone had, it is believed, 163,000 Swiss in his armies. The great Protestant reformer Huldrych Zwingli opposed this — and all mercenary activity — and convinced his native city, Zurich, to resist traditional mercenary arrangements. But many of the Swiss cantons were so dependent on mercenary service as an outlet for overpopulation and as a source of external remittances that they resisted his proposed restrictions. Numerous Swiss would therefore continue to fight in the battles of Europe for centuries to come. But Switzerland itself as a nation withdrew from what had earlier seemed almost a fated role as a major military player in European politics and began its policy of independence and neutrality just as the major nations of Europe were taking on the basic forms they have had for the past half millennium.

Renewed Swiss Commitment to the Pope

The Swiss still had a pact with the pope. And he soon called on them for several purposes. The first was to send forces to defend Italy again. The commander of the Swiss Guard had gone to Switzerland in 1517 and come back to northern Italy with men he had recruited. In August of that year, he was in Rimini waiting to meet up with the papal army accompanied by two hundred Swiss guards and about another fifteen hundred Swiss troops. They were caught in a surprise attack at night by the forces of Francesco Maria della Rovere, whom the pope had deposed as duke of Urbino and replaced with one of his own Medici relatives. After four hours of furious battle, the Swiss drove back the invaders and retook the city, very nearly capturing the duke. But their founding commander, Kaspar von Silenen, who had served two popes over more than ten years, died in the conflict.[6] Von Silenen was given a solemn funeral in Rome, though there is no record of where he was buried. Johannes Faber, the prior of the Dominican monastery at Augsburg and a famous humanist, happened to be in Rome at the time and gave a moving eulogy. The Swiss had lost their only commander to date but had managed to show their value in their defense of papal interests.

At the same period, however, a still greater threat presented itself. The Turks were taking control of Egypt and Syria, and Leo, as had other popes before him, called on Christians to unite in the face of the Muslim menace. As had also happened before, the various rulers ignored the plea or excused themselves because of immediate national interests. In order to be able to lead the effort himself, Leo asked the Swiss for an additional twelve thousand men. Ten thousand were approved by the Swiss authorities but never departed for Rome because of uncertainties over the impending election of a new Holy Roman Emperor. The Swiss hesitated because they believed they might need men to defend themselves from the new emperor, as they had in the past. Fortunately for all concerned, Muslim forces did not launch a major new assault on the vulnerable lands in Western Europe just yet.

In the meantime, the Swiss Guard faced a problem of succession. Who would be the next commander? Kaspar von Silenen's brother Christoph, who was then a lieutenant in the Guard, would have been a natural choice and put himself forward as a candidate. The guards themselves wanted to exercise their ancient rights, which stipulated that a body of Swiss soldiers could select their own leader. But because of various intrigues, the von Silenen family could not continue in the post. In moves that probably had more to do with politics than authentic law, they had been marginalized back in Switzerland (Kaspar had been convicted in absentia of violating rules prohibiting recruitment of mercenaries for the pope), their lands were confiscated, and their influence all but eliminated. The pope's representative reported to Leo on all these facts. The Hertenstein family, which was closely related to the von Silenens (Peter von Hertenstein, as we have seen, had been instrumental in the creation of the Guard), might have been the next choice. But at the moment they were primarily in the service of the French, who were enemies of the pope. It would have been inviting trouble for members of the same family to enlist in armies that might face each other in the field.

Kaspar Röist's Reform of the Guard

The choice fell on a distinguished military man and political figure: Marx (Marcus) Röist, who became mayor of Zurich in 1505 and had been one of the commanders at the disastrous battle of Marignano, where he was seriously wounded. But Marcus had come to oppose mercenary services and, in any case, at sixty-two could not see his way clear to leave Zurich. The papal legate and others pleaded with him that it would be "ingratitude to God and Homeland" for him to refuse. A solution was finally found. He would be titular head of the Swiss Guard and would have to serve in Rome only for a month or two. Then his son would carry out the actual duties. Marcus agreed, but asked for the arrangements to be confirmed in writing by the Zurich council and the Vatican. Even this solution was subject to further negotiations. Marcus at first designated his son Diethelm for the task. When the day came, however, another son, Kaspar, who was then forty, accompanied him instead. Father and son set off for Rome on February 23, 1518, but Marcus had to turn back because of sudden illness. Whether this was an authentic malady or part of a prearranged plan remains unknown. Kaspar arrived by himself in Rome toward the end of March with instructions from Zurich that he was to exercise functions as both a diplomat at the Roman Curia and officer in the Swiss Guard. This was the beginning of a dual function for the commander of the Swiss Guard that would endure for some time.

Röist seems to have been one of those men blessed with multiple gifts, including great leadership skills. He carried out both charges admirably. A graduate of the University of Basel, he was quite well educated. Growing up in the distinguished family that he did, he was familiar with political, economic, and military matters from a relatively early age. His own immediate family would be intimately linked with Rome for years. Five of his six children were to be born there. Röist adroitly handled Swiss diplomatic questions in Rome, whether they involved political or religious issues. But he was notably distinguished for his reforms of the Guard as well, turning it into a truly elite corps again and recognized by everyone as such. This was not an easy task. Discipline had slipped in the period before he arrived, and it was difficult for him to put it on a firm footing again. When he tried to get rid of some of the worst cases among his troops, for example, he had to bow to the wishes of the Zurich council and reinstate them. Röist managed to turn this overruling of his own wishes into a conspicuous example of military obedience and thereby set a personal standard for the guards.

Somehow he also gained the trust and support of Christoph von Silenen, the first commander's brother, who might have been expected to resent the new commander, who had been appointed over his own ambitions. Von Silenen was of great help in earning the respect and goodwill of a good portion of the men toward Röist. But others seemed to have degenerated almost beyond reform. Some guards, taking advantage of their proximity to high Church officials, had become virtual courtiers, scheming for benefices and preferments in the Church. Such ambitions were obviously in conflict with the military character of the Swiss Guard. This problem had already arisen under Julius II, but no easy remedy for it seemed available. In 1520, two guards competing for a benefice back in Switzerland actually came to blows, and one was wounded. Röist knew that he either had to break up this unhealthy situation or the guards would be simply unsuitable for the duties with which they had been entrusted.

Röist carefully calculated each step, but shrewdly, forcefully, relentlessly he reintroduced discipline, and, by 1523, the Swiss guards were back in tiptop military form and universally admired again. Long before that, however, Röist's labors came to the attention of Pope Leo. He found the commander's work so valuable that he promised him a house with a vineyard near the Belvedere in the Vatican. But Leo was to die on December 1, 1521, and the cardinals who took over management of the Church let stand the promise in the Vatican's account books without taking any action to honor it.[7]

Leo X's Death and Its Consequences

Leo's death left the affairs of the Church in grave uncertainty. For some years he had feared plots from the cardinals in Rome, and therefore always moved about with a significant number of Swiss guards. As is the case with the guards even today, this sometimes stretched manpower beyond what was humanly manageable. Commandant Röist went so far as to write to the Zurich council that five hundred, not the usual two hundred, Swiss might be needed both for the pope's purposes and to keep them from exhaustion. Furthermore, the pope had to calculate his military needs for three possible political scenarios: war with France; war to expel the Spanish from Naples; or an alliance with France against the Habsburgs who ruled the Holy Roman Empire. When Charles V, the Spanish king, was chosen as the Holy Roman Emperor in 1519, Leo's decision became very easy. The newly combined power of Spain and the empire was by far the greatest threat.

Leo set about organizing an alliance with France against Charles and the Habsburgs. But the pope was good neither at deciding on a course of action nor on sticking to it. He sent his trusted former nuncio to Switzerland, Bishop Antonio Pucci of Pistoia, to recruit six thousand Swiss. It took two years, but Pucci returned in 1521 with the requested number and an additional four thousand unpaid volunteers who expected to get booty out of the war. The troops were assembled near the eastern port of Ancona. But when no papal orders were forthcoming Pucci and a number of the Swiss commanders rode to Rome. There they were received with great honors and celebrations, but the pope now thought that since the Spanish threat had not materialized, maybe the Swiss should go back home — or at least the unpaid volunteers should do so. One of the Swiss commanders, Kaspar Göldli of Zurich, rode back to the troops, where he received an even more surprising message. Now the pope wanted the whole army to return home. Whether this reversal was the result of the absence of enemy activity, of Leo's inability to pay for so large a host, or of another simple change of mind on his part is difficult to say. Most of the troops turned north.

The pope asked Göldli for some reinforcements for his Swiss guards. The planning for this second group, however, was as makeshift as the pope's thinking about the larger army. Two hundred new guards arrived in Rome. For some reason, they were housed away from the Vatican, where they could have done the most good, in the area known as Trastevere. They even had a separate commander, Bartleme Berweger, though they wore the same uniforms as the guards stationed at the Vatican. The pope had good reason to think he needed extra guards, since the cardinals and leading citizens of Rome had designs against him because of the unpredictability of his policies and his quick emptying of the papal treasury. These Roman enemies, too, would become a central factor in events leading to the sack of the city.

Meanwhile, there were still about two thousand Swiss troops in northern Italy, who began campaigns on their own. They took Ferrara and defeated the French, driving them back to their two strongholds in Cremona and Milan. Leo seems to have forgotten for the moment that he had earlier planned to make an alliance with the French against the combined Spanish and imperial forces under Charles V, because he celebrated these victories without, it seems, worrying about the future consequences. His own Swiss guards, however, took particular satisfaction in these victories, regarding them as revenge for the infamous and bloody defeat at Marignano a few years earlier at the hands of the French. They lit bonfires and celebrated all night. The pope watched them with approval from an open window. But it was late November, a cold month in Rome, and the pope's health was not robust. He contracted a malarial fever and died five days later on December 1, 1521.

Pope Adrian VI and Early Reformation Politics

The guards kept order around the Vatican in the interim between Leo's death and the choice of his successor. Before the Guard came into existence, this interim period had often been a time of disorder and looting in Rome. But the guards got little credit for their trouble. Since by the terms of their service oaths, they had been loyal to the Medici family, the cardinals who met in the conclave to select the new pope did not trust them and ordered one thousand Italian soldiers to stand by. Naturally, the Swiss took this as an insult and a form of dishonor to their sworn service. When a Dutchman was elected as Adrian VI on January 9, 1522, the cardinals disbanded the second Swiss Guard troops quartered in Trastevere. It seemed briefly that the main body of the guards, too, might no longer be needed by the new pope. But in fact, they were highly recommended to the pope by the cardinals for their courage and loyalty to the Church.[8]

The dismissal of the Trastevere guards, however, caused a stir and no little anger back in Zurich. Their ill treatment, along with the growing Protestant movement under the leadership of Zwingli, put the guards in a precarious situation. Zwingli, oddly, began as part of the papal party because he opposed alliances with other nations. And he was among the leaders of the Zurich majority who refused military capitulation and the peace treaty with France in 1521. But when Charles V was elected emperor, this created a special situation, since the emperor was an energetic leader who seemed likely to try to unite all of Christendom again in a universal monarchy. And there was no telling what that might mean for Swiss independence. In addition, it was difficult even for the Swiss in Rome to appreciate the depth of the changes occurring under Zwingli's religious influence in Zurich. They seemed to most people little more than a passing crisis. But the whole situation threatened to spin out of control since Zwingli and his followers in Switzerland had their own interests now and felt no great obligation to the hated leader of the Church in Rome.

Around this time, a Swiss ban on all foreign military service was passed, which also seemed to deny the legitimacy of the Swiss guards in Rome, and their commander was aware of the potentially explosive nature of the situation. Röist went to Zurich with the papal nuncio to try to get some clarity about their status. The Zurich council simply sent him back to Adrian VI with a letter describing him as "Your Holiness's Commandant." The larger question of the guards' status was not settled, but for the time being the old arrangements seemed to have been reaffirmed by the Swiss. Adrian himself, however, seemed unwilling to leave well enough alone. At one point, he requested that twenty-four Spaniards be admitted to the guards. It is not clear why he did so, but the arrangement by its very nature could not last. In short order, the strict discipline and foreign living conditions caused them to resign.[9]

The new pope did not last long himself, only about eighteen months. Adrian VI died on September 14, 1523, a holy man, but hated by the Romans for his neglect of the business side of the Church and his inability to make anything happen while the Turks conquered Belgrade and Rhodes. The Dutch pope had been elected only because two Italian families, the Colonna and the Medici, blocked one another's aspirations, and no other compromise candidate had been found. In the conclave that met after Adrian's death, the two main Italian families were also backed by opposing political factions aligned with the king of France on the one hand (Medici) and the Holy Roman Empire and Charles V of Spain on the other (Colonna). The French cardinals had ridden hard to Rome in order to be present in time to stop an unwanted result. As all the cardinals settled into their deliberations, the Romans began to agitate outside, as was their custom at the time, and the Roman commune even threatened to starve out the cardinals unless they decided quickly. Most observers thought Cardinal Alessandro Farnese, a Roman popular among the Romans, who also exuded great authority, might be the best choice the gathered princes of the Church could make.

Clement VII and the First Threats to Rome

That was not to be. Whether by the inspiration of the Holy Spirit or by political intrigue, or both, Giulio de' Medici became Pope Clement VII on November 19, 1523, about five weeks after the threats against the cardinals. But Clement turned out to be more like Adrian VI than his opulent cousin, Pope Leo X. Leo had known how to use the pomp and pageantry of the papacy to impress the Roman people. Clement, like Adrian, was rather bookish and indecisive. Some claimed he was also the most accomplished musician in all of Italy at the time. He actually fasted rigorously during Lent and possessed a measure of real personal holiness. Instead of jesters at the papal court, he preferred "the company of learned doctors with whom he discussed health-foods and good diets, of philosophers and theologians who were required to discourse on their own subjects while the pope ate."[10] This sort of man was not particularly suited to the rough-and-tumble conditions of Rome and Italy in the sixteenth century. He often used the old Florentine principle of delaying as long as possible when he did not know what to do, but the challenges he faced often required swift and vigorous action. The Reformation perspective on the Church in the Renaissance has tended to obscure the fact that there were good and holy popes like Clement and Adrian at the time. But in the circumstances, it is difficult to say whether they were good for Rome and Italy.

In some obvious ways, of course, they were. Papal Rome had already been a great patron of all the arts before Clement's election, and that along with Rome's historical prestige made the city the natural leader of Italy and, to a certain degree, of all Europe. Many pilgrims, classical enthusiasts, artists, and art collectors came to Rome in a steady stream. Jubilee years temporarily swelled the already large numbers. Even if the artistic and imperial elements had gone to seed under the Borgias, Julius II, and Leo X — which shocked consciences like Luther's during his visit to the Eternal City in the early 1500s — Rome exerted an undeniable fascination for good and ill all over Europe.

In the 1520s, Rome was beginning to grow beautiful again. The new St. Peter's, started by Pope Julius II, was making progress, despite opposition from near and far, if at a very slow pace. The various neighborhoods (*borgos*) surrounding the Vatican began to take on more attractive shape, and wider thoroughfares replaced tangled medieval streets and alleys — largely at Clement VII's initiative. New palaces incorporating classical features and designed by famous artists such as Bramante and Giulio Romano arose owing to the wealth of families such as the Orsini, Giberti, Strozzi, Cenci, and many others. Statues, paintings, jewelry, manuscripts, books, and small works of art were present and for sale everywhere. The Sapienza University building, based on a design by Michelangelo, was completed in the heart of the old city not far from Piazza Navona. Artists like Raphael and many others, of course, had been working to beautify the city for decades. Large numbers of Jews had fled persecution in Iberia and southern France for the Roman *ghetto* and, along with settlers from all over Europe, especially Spain and Germany (potential problems), created a decidedly cosmopolitan atmosphere within the city's confines. In short, while there were certainly plenty of problems in the Church and Papal States at the time of Clement VII's election, he took command over a city that was in many ways the center of the European world.

Yet there were many ways, also, in which all of this apparent cultural richness was hollow and, more seriously, vulnerable. As king of Spain and Holy Roman Emperor, Charles V commanded the most potent political and military forces in Europe including the Netherlands, second only to Italy in its wealth. His major concerns did not, at least immediately, include a desire to conquer Italy, but to stop the Turks first of all, who were moving west again. Next, he had to counter the growing power of France, a real rival. Finally, he wanted to contain Martin Luther's reformation since it threatened order in Germany. Charles V resented Clement VII partly because he had failed to do anything about these problems and had even entered into an alliance with Venice, Milan, France, and other powers to stop his advance. But there were inherent tensions, as there often had been in the past, between popes and all rulers. And it was only natural that Charles came to believe that by conquering Italy and controlling the papacy he would improve his chances to deal with what he regarded as the three real threats he faced.

The wealth of Italy would also help with another problem for both the empire and France. Since neither power had the full resources needed for the armies they had to send out, a place such as Italy offered ample opportunities for daily provisions along the way and for outright plunder. Indeed, even the pope did not have sufficient revenues to pay his own forces and had to resort to unpopular taxes to try meeting the need. In the aftermath of the sack of Rome, many parties — among them Charles V himself — would lament the damage to the first city of Christendom. By then, however, a pattern had been established that would lead directly to the sad result. Charles also intrigued with his allies, the Colonna, in Rome and the various segments of Roman society that had come to resent the papal levies on their financial transactions. Had that avenue worked, perhaps an invasion of Italy would not have been deemed necessary and much bloodshed would have been avoided. But as it turned out, the sack of Rome was the culmination of a chain of events set in motion much earlier.

Charles V's Moves in Italy

In 1525, for example, Charles V won a massive victory near the northern Italian city of Pavia, in which he captured the king of France himself. As the battle began, however, the emperor already owed his army six hundred thousand ducats. Paradoxically, this offered an advantage to the territories he threatened. He was inclined to make deals with them if they would make large payments to his treasury. Florence and the pope each agreed to pay out a hundred thousand ducats for certain concessions. Smaller Italian political entities offered more modest amounts. But the ruler of Milan, Francesco Sforza, pledged six hundred thousand ducats to redeem his territory and regain his leadership. Many people argued then and since that these agreements might have spared Italy from harrowing experiences. But they were not to be honored.

Clement VII quietly formed a broad and extensive alliance — the Italian League — to oppose Charles. Among other things, the pope feared that the emperor wanted to call a general council to depose him and install another pope pliant to his wishes. And in this he was exactly right. Charles wanted civil peace and an end to religious controversy so that he could focus his energies on fighting the Turks. He needed to pacify various parts of Europe, and, he thought, he needed a pope who could better deal with the growing Protestant fever. The members of the Italian League were not exactly supporters of Clement, but the threat of Spanish invasion brought large parts of Italy together again for the first time since the fall of the ancient Roman Empire in a loose but real Italian desire for liberty.

Clement had some of the greatest figures in Italy at his command. Francesco Guicciardini, Machiavelli's great Florentine contemporary who, like Machiavelli, was both a thinker and a man of action, was appointed lieutenant-general of the pope's army. Clement's ambassador in Spain for a while was another great literary figure, Baldassare Castiglione, whose book *Il Cortegiano* (The Courtier) was the essential guide to behavior for aspiring gentlemen. But Castiglione was very much pro-Spanish, and his presence at the Spanish court may not have been as effective on Clement's behalf as it could have been.

Spain's own ambassadors to Clement were willing to negotiate and even to make some large concessions. But Clement was constrained by his financial situation to resist the kinds of agreements they proposed. As we have seen, this central problem of his papacy largely originated within his own family. Leo X, his cousin, had lived quite lavishly and was much liked by the Romans for it, since he provided all sorts of different people with a steady livelihood. But Leo had bankrupted the papacy and run the treasury into deep debt to gain popularity. So the papacy in the new Rome, outwardly prosperous to the eye, possessed in fact very modest resources, and some of Clement's obstinacy in dealing with imperial representatives stemmed from the fact that he simply could not pay what he was being asked to pay.

At the same time, he could not afford not to keep his armies and other retainers in good order. Ambassadors found their salaries and operating budgets cut. The Swiss guards themselves were not being paid and occasionally had to find other odd jobs to make a living. To deal with these fiscal challenges, Clement used the banks of his fellow Florentines, who were already numerous in the city. This helped because they charged him relatively low interest rates on loans, but that meant that the traditional Roman bankers suffered. Clement was honestly trying to fix a problem he did not create. He could have sold cardinalships and reaped the financial benefits but was morally against such expedients. Instead, he increased taxes on wine, meat, and other common products and reaped the hatred of the Romans. Imperial agents, operating through Roman families such as the Colonna, who hated the Medici, secretly stirred up discontent. So Clement was not exactly the real cause of the ills that befell him and the Church, but as is often the case in public life, he was unpopular and regarded as ineffectual because he could not solve the problems bequeathed to him by a popular predecessor. And Charles V threatened him directly and indirectly by encouraging dissent among the cardinals.

The Colonna and the First Sack of Rome

The leader of this dissent was Cardinal Pompeio Colonna (the Colonna family were traditionally aligned with Spain against the Orsini, who were allied to Florence and France). Colonna military forces sought to take advantage of the fact that Clement's army (though not the Swiss Guard) had been disbanded, leaving him with only about five hundred defenders, and that his treasury was empty. Supported by about five thousand foot soldiers and six hundred mounted knights, Cardinal Colonna entered Rome in

September of 1526 unopposed and marched through the streets without hindrance in a kind of triumphal procession. Clement had called upon the populace to rise up, but there was no response. The Colonna troops crossed the Tiber into Trastevere and then began to go upriver toward the Vatican. Clement ordered his main protectors, the Swiss Guard, to take up defensive positions, which included manning the artillery in Castel Sant'Angelo. A small force of about one hundred other soldiers stopped the initial advance of the Colonna troops at Porta Santo Spirito, the gate that can still be seen behind the hospital of Santo Spirito.

The Colonna officers saw that they would suffer many casualties by further direct attack on the gate and decided to storm a broken part of the wall instead. Pope Clement decided "to die on his throne," but was eventually convinced by various supporters to flee.[11] In a kind of dress rehearsal for the later and greater assault, Clement took the specially built passage along the top of the Vatican wall to Castel Sant'Angelo. In another anticipation of what was to come in even greater proportions later, the Colonna soldiers began to sack the Vatican, though the Swiss Guard brought forward a dozen cannons and were able to keep them from certain parts of the area. Unfortunately, Clement ordered them to fall back, even as they were driving back the enemy, and accompany him to the castle. The sack of the Colonna (*Sacco dei Colonna*), as it is sometimes called, thus began again and even included the living quarters of the Swiss. It appears, however, that more than greed was involved in the ransacking of the Leonine City. There was also a deliberate attempt to find diplomatic correspondence and other papal documents that might reveal Clement's arrangements with Italian and European powers. This information would have been useful to several parties, including Cardinal Colonna. But it is clear that there must have been another hand behind the operation, that of the Emperor Charles V.

Poor Pope Clement faced another threat as well. Castel Sant' Angelo was for all intents and purposes at the time a secure fortress — if it was fully prepared. It had not been. Giulio de' Medici, a relative in charge of the castle as castellan, had not done his job properly. Partly this was the result of Clement's general attempts to save money. But it was also partly owing to sheer ineptness on Giulio's part. This forced a parley between the pope and the Colonna officers. The Spanish ambassador Ugo Moncada demanded the surrender of the castle. Clement could not surrender without effectively allowing the emperor free rein in Rome and perhaps central Italy. Moncada had his own heavy artillery brought up and aimed at the fortress to put further pressure on Clement.

The deal that was eventually struck was partly unsatisfactory to all sides. Clement remained in power and the Colonna forces withdrew. But the pope agreed to a cease-fire in the most important areas of the Italian peninsula and a withdrawal of papal forces from those conflicts to positions within the Papal States. In return, Moncada withdrew his forces from the papal territories. He had expected much popular support for the attempt to unseat the unpopular Clement. But it did not materialize. Instead, many Italians all over the peninsula who might have in the past thought Clement an inept ruler who needed to be replaced now began to fear that the emperor wanted complete control over Italy. And their fears were further inflamed by the Colonnas' claim that the emperor had ordered the raid. Popular opinion in Rome itself was so changed by the experience that when a rumor of another attack by the Colonna arose in early October, Romans took to the streets shouting "For the Church," and "Long Live Pope Clement."[12]

The raid also revealed that Clement was not as entirely inept as believed. He had already ordered reinforcements for the Vatican before the raid occurred. And in good Machiavellian fashion, he took his time in complying with the terms of his truce, even arranging it so that certain papal troops around Milan would continue to be paid from Rome while fighting under the nominal leadership of the French. So the Italian League against the Spanish threat had not suffered grave reversals, and Clement intended to continue working with it. Indeed, situated as he was between Naples and the northern powers, he had a clearer sense of the peninsula-wide threat than did several of his important allies, notably Florence and Venice, who took a more self-interested view. But the raid also revealed several vulnerabilities among the papal forces, which Clement's enemies would later exploit.

Clement's options were still limited by his financial situation. He repeatedly warned France and Venice that he would have to accept a truce with Spain if they did not support him financially. They disliked the idea, thinking it a bad deal for all concerned. Clement agreed, but made a deal with the imperial representative Lannoy on March 15, 1527: "I know it is a bad thing to make a truce, and it is also a bad thing to make war; but to make the truce seems the lesser evil."[13] The imperial forces may have felt mostly the same. While they, too, continued preparing for an assault on Rome, they were faced with constant threats of mutiny owing to lack of pay. Indeed, reading the military history of the period sometimes becomes more a wearisome record of debts and expedients to pay thousands of troops rather than of military valor and achievement. Scrambling to find ways to pay large armies was a common problem in the age for all parties. And the result was that financial payments included in agreements were usually no more than a temporary solution to the immediate situation. This fact added to the common inclination to break truces when it was expedient anyway.

Zurich's Recall of the Swiss

Amid all this turmoil, the Swiss Guard faced an internal question of its own. On January 20, 1527, the Zurich council issued an order that all the guards from Zurich should return home within four months. Commandant Röist gathered those men together and read them the letter. They all agreed that they could not desert their post and leave the pope — or their comrades — in the lurch when such danger threatened on all sides.[14] Röist communicated this decision, which was his own as well, to Zurich, adding that as soon as there was peace, he would return home. But till then he could not ignore his responsibilities to God and honor. It was a fateful step.

That declaration by the Swiss, made in the knowledge that remaining at their posts might mean their own death warrants, was certainly sincere. But the prospects for peace were dim, even if the leaders had been able to reach some agreement. It had become the common view among the many foreign soldiers roaming around Italy that the only way they would ever get full monetary satisfaction was to go down to Rome and loot the city. This was spoken of openly. And a group of imperial captains even made a thinly veiled threat to a papal envoy, telling him that "many of their men, and indeed almost all, were in a state of mortal sin and wanted to go to Rome to gain absolution; and that for such a expedition they had not asked and would not ask for a penny in pay."[15] The imperial representative Lannoy and the duke of Bourbon, another imperial commander, skillfully used threats of this kind to extort money from the pope and his allies, such as Florence. And all the evidence points to the fact that despite some public confusion of who was actually in charge — a deliberate tactic of Charles V's — they had private assurances from the emperor that he would support them in whatever they wanted to do in Italy.

So Clement's willingness under duress to accept the truce was partly a matter of wishful thinking on his part. The imperial representatives were Machiavellians, just waiting for the right moment for treachery. France and Venice were furious with the pope for making a bad deal and sought a new alliance of their own to try to stop imperial advances. Clement sent an ambassador to the Venetians to explain. But the Venetian doge simply replied to him, "This pope will be the ruin of all Italy."[16]

The ruin soon began. Imperial forces under the command of the duke of Bourbon literally cut a swath through the forests in the countryside surrounding Bologna and continued moving south, looting and burning towns and homes along the way. As they approached Florence, firmly in control of the pope and his family, anti-Medici forces planned an internal uprising to meet them. Even the Medici supporters had been weakened in their allegiance by the lessening of the benefits they had enjoyed under Clement's cousin, Pope Leo X. Some from the more prominent families thought the invasion inevitable and fled for safe havens elsewhere, believing that the advancing armies would doubtless sack the fabled wealth of the city. In the so-called "Friday Riot," a mixed band of anti-Medici and formerly pro-Medici forces — including some of the most prominent Florentine families such as the Salviati, Capponi, Alemanni, Strozzi, and others — began agitating. Abetted by the Colonnas in Rome and the advancing duke of Bourbon, they occupied the Palazzo della Signoria, Florence's seat of government. They were soon persuaded by the intervention of Francesco Guicciardini and others to relent by promises of total amnesty. But their agitation showed the depth of anxiety within the city and how easily it could erupt into instability. The plotters had wanted the uprising to lead to an opening of the city gates to the invaders. The failure of the uprising led the duke of Bourbon to give up his intention of taking Florence and to direct his army — who only reluctantly gave up the chance of ransacking the city — directly toward Rome down the ancient Roman Via Cassia.

The Colonna had prepared a plan for the invasion of Rome as well. Their supporters would try to stir up popular rebellion, and on May 10 would open the gate that most visitors then passed through when entering the city from the north, the Porta del Popolo. But the imperial troops moved so quickly that they were just a few miles away by early May, and the duke of Bourbon could not afford to hold his men back. The preponderance of the evidence seems to indicate that at least he personally did not intend to let his troops ransack Rome. He wanted only to capture the pope and force him to pay a large sum. But it was not the first time in war that circumstances led to deeds that outran limits placed upon them ahead of time.

The 1527 Sack of Rome

Though in retrospect the outcome seems inevitable, it was rare at the time for heavily fortified cities to be broken into. And doing so without artillery was even more rare. The duke of Bourbon had had to leave his heavy guns along the difficult way, and replacements from the Colonnas had not yet materialized. And the conditions of his army were such that even a delay of a few days would exhaust their supplies. Even more worrisome for the commander of the army, allowing soldiers to loot almost always led to the utter breakdown of discipline. For all his reputation as an inept leader, Clement tried to take advantage of such possibilities as existed in his desperate situation. He raised money from the Romans by promising not to abandon the city. At a large General Council in the Ara Coeli church on the Capitoline Hill, he pointed out that if the city could hold off the attackers for a few days they would be in a good position. And he volunteered to give up the relative safety of Castel Sant'Angelo and live in Palazzo Venezia, relatively exposed in Rome's center, during the conflict.

Defenses were set up and succeeded in the first forays. When one boatload of imperial soldiers tried to cross the Tiber, for example, they were quickly sunk. But the imperial troops were desperate and saw the city as their only relief. The duke of Bourbon spurred them on by telling the Catholics that failure would bring punishment from the pope. To his Lutherans, he held out the chance to kill priests and bishops. And so various circumstances conspired to bring about the clash on May 6, 1527. The imperialists attacked again at Santo Spirito. But the artillery of the Swiss Guard from Castel Sant'Angelo was quite effective in disrupting the invaders, and five imperial banners were captured. In a great stroke of luck for the papal forces, the duke of Bourbon himself was shot by an arquebus and killed as he tried to climb a ladder over the city walls. The news spread quickly and the defenders momentarily felt that victory might be within their grasp.

But it was not to be. They were vastly outnumbered and the attackers knew something about warfare. For the most part, the hastily mustered and thrown together Roman defenders did not. The main assault took place near Santo Spirito and the area near St. Peter's that, today, is the Via delle Fornaci. When the city walls were breached, the defenders fled for their homes. The Swiss Guard and the Roman militia were basically the only real resistance as the numerous attackers advanced. The fighting became savage. Commandant Röist led the defenses at the Porta delle Fornaci, but, like his imperial counterpart, also fell. As one historian describes it: "The Swiss had taken up their position near the obelisk, then still standing near the Campo Santo, and they were cut to pieces. Their captain, Röist, was carried, gravely wounded, into his own house and laid gently on his own bed, where, a few minutes later, he was slaughtered before the eyes of his wife by soldiers who had broken into the house."[17] In fact, Röist's wife tried to shield the wounded man with her own person, and three of her fingers were cut off when Spanish soldiers hacked away at his body. All the guards who had fought with him to defend the main point where the imperial forces had attacked, 147 of them, perished. Before they fell, they killed about 900 of the invaders.

The pope was at Mass during this assault and had to be evacuated. His flight came just in the nick of time. A minute or two later, according to some observers, he would have been captured. Clement was so weak that a special contingent of forty-two Swiss assigned to protect his person during the assault had to carry him down the special passageway from the Vatican to Castel Sant'Angelo, now under the orders of the Swiss next-in-command, Herkules Göldli. Bishop Paolo Giovio of Nocera held a cloak over the pontiff to shield him from view. Amazingly, the castle had not been prepared for siege any more than it was during the Colonna raid. Provisions were brought in hastily. People pressed in seeking refuge themselves from the slaughter. Their numbers were so large that the drawbridge had to be raised in spite of the fact that many were still on it. Of these and others, not a few wound up in the moat.

Inside Castel Sant'Angelo, the pope could not have had a very good idea of what was going on in Rome or elsewhere. Almost a thousand people, including 350 soldiers — the few surviving Swiss guards among them — were inside the castle walls. Accommodations were tight, but there was sufficient food and drink for a month and plenty of ammunition and powder for the artillery that had always been the castle's most important defensive feature. Imperial forces dealt brutally with anyone who tried to approach the castle, even killing an old woman bringing lettuce as a gift to the pope.[18] But the papal side did not entirely lose heart. Surprisingly, religious disciplines were kept up so that many who participated in them remarked that the atmosphere was somewhat similar to a retreat in a religious house. But even allowing for the best interpretation of the situation, the papal side was stuck, and while it could refuse humiliating demands by a desperate imperial siege, there was little more it could do than keep up discipline and morale, defend the ramparts — and wait.

Chapter Four

Siege, Dissolution, Rebirth

From street level, the Castel Sant'Angelo is not very impressive. It certainly offers a close-up view of the kinds of battlements and bastions you might expect to find in an ancient fortress. But it possesses none of the interest of a truly fine ancient or modern building, or of a Renaissance jewel like St. Peter's, a masterpiece that architectural historians have studied exhaustively. The "castle" is the result of medieval and Renaissance extensions of a previously existing round structure with an unexceptional statue of the Archangel Michael, after whom the Castel Sant'Angelo is named, on top. The Ponte degli Angeli that leads across the Tiber River to the castle is a pleasant walk, in its modern form, with large and graceful Bernini angels on either side. Yet many people visit Rome today and see the castle near the Vatican without feeling any curiosity about the rather forbidding brick mass, even though, despite all appearances, the castle played a central role in the history of Rome over the centuries.

Only after entering and starting to climb the broad, gradual internal ramps toward the top, which were built so high and wide that a chariot can be driven up them, do the truly pharaonic proportions of the castle — and their uses as a stronghold — become clear. In fact, it feels very much as if you were climbing up the inside of one of the Egyptian pyramids, and with good reason. The original round structure was a massive mausoleum for the Roman emperor Hadrian, one of the "good" emperors (Antoninus Pius and the great Marcus Aurelius were also buried here) during the second century after Christ's death. It was built on so large a scale that, in its original layout, it was a kind of artificial hill with what amounted to a whole grove of trees planted on its flat summit with a huge statue of the emperor driving a four-horse chariot in their midst. Later additions replaced all that. Still, there is a kind of wistfulness about it to this day. Hadrian is famous for having written a little poem shortly before his death:

> *Animula vagula blandula*
> *hospes comesque corporis*
> *quae nunc abibis in loca*
> *pallidula rigida nudula*
> *nec ut soles dabis iocos!*

> Little pale wandering soul
> Guest and companion of the body,
> Now you must depart for places
> Pallid and rigid and naked,
> And you will not make your usual jokes!

Ironically, the tomb of this Roman ruler was erected between AD 130 and 140 in what the ancient Romans called the Campus Martius (Field of Mars) not far from the spot where tradition says the prince of the apostles, St. Peter, suffered martyrdom and was buried (underneath the main altar of St. Peter's Basilica).

In spite of its original purpose as a place of repose, Castel Sant'Angelo played a very active part in the life of Rome during the Middles Ages and Renaissance. In fact, one historian has rightly said that "the history of the Mausoleum in the Middle Ages is almost the history of Rome."[1] Though it seems that the classical structure was kept more or less intact for about three hundred years, it was turned into a fortress in the fifth century, as the barbarians were putting pressure on what remained of the ancient Roman Empire. During a fifth-century invasion, the old Romans themselves were driven into what we now call Castel Sant'Angelo and were forced *in extremis* to throw down the many classical statues that once decorated the building onto the besiegers. Over the next several centuries, the marble facings were stripped, and the stone for the emperors' tombs was adapted for other purposes. Towers, ramparts, and walls were added that made the castle virtually impregnable.

A deeper connection with the city of Rome is reflected in a strange thing that happened in 590 that gave the castle its name. During a plague that struck Rome after a flood the previous year, Pope Gregory the Great organized a procession to pray for deliverance. According to legend, as he was crossing the bridge near the castle on the way to St. Peter's, the pope had a vision of an archangel on the summit putting a bloody sword back into its sheath. That angel was surrounded by other angels who were singing what has, in the centuries since, become a popular Catholic hymn, the "Regina coeli": *Regina coeli laetare, quia quem meruisti portare, resurrexit, sicut dixit, Alleluia* (Queen of heaven rejoice, because he whom you deserved to bear has arisen, as he said, Alleluia). Whatever we might make of that episode today, there is a long tradition from the biblical book of Chronicles ("And God sent an angel to Jerusalem to destroy it...") down to the plague that struck London in the seventeenth century of associating angels of destruction with catastrophes. In 608, Pope Boniface IV built a chapel dedicated to St. Michael the archangel on top of the castle. Nearly a thousand years later, the statue of the angel was added.

A Renaissance Fortress and Palace

The Renaissance popes also added outworks to make approaches by land extremely difficult. At that point, the fortress had guard towers and walls that brought it right to the banks of the Tiber River, which made attack from that direction impossible. All this has to be imagined clearly to appreciate the situation in which the pope and his Swiss guards found themselves in 1527. Much of the more fearsome side of Castel Sant'Angelo has since disappeared. The neighborhoods have been planted with trees and wide walkways and avenues introduced. Today, there is even a café on one of the upper levels of the building where tourists sip cappuccino looking out at the whole panorama of Rome through the arched windows that used to hold cannons. But this is not wholly out of keeping with the castle's history. Even at the point when it was most configured for military purposes, it also contained some comforts for the use of the pope and the Curia. Now, several museums dedicated to papal life and military history are housed in some of those rooms. Amid the historical exhibits, there are still examples of the weapons and uniforms of the sixteenth-century guards, which, repaired and polished up, could probably be used by their contemporary descendants without the average person noticing very much difference. From the heights of the tower, it is not difficult to see why many invaders found it impregnable. The four bastions — built by Pope Nicholas V in the century prior to the imperial invasion — are named, perhaps somewhat blasphemously, after the four evangelists: Matthew, Mark, Luke, and John. Any assault on this brick mass would have been nothing less than suicide.

The Atmosphere during the Siege

We do not know precisely what the feelings of the pope and his guards may have been as they sat atop all this history in the state of siege. The religious atmosphere mentioned in the previous chapter no doubt predominated in public, but anxiety must have gnawed away in private just beneath the surface. The Swiss had lost about three-quarters of their comrades in a single day, including the commander. Panic had been so sudden and deep throughout the city that various church and secular officials, along with the ambassadors of France and England, and three thousand assorted souls had crammed into the castle. Cardinal Armellini, who apparently had been left outside when the drawbridge was raised, had to be lifted in a basket to safety within the fortress walls.

But any safety in the circumstance was only relative and might shortly prove illusory. Although precise knowledge of what was happening in the city below was difficult to get, we know from several sources that the defenders had a clear view of the outrages perpetrated by the imperial troops. Raffaello da Montelupo, a sculptor who had found refuge in the castle, recorded the helplessness they felt: "We stood there and looked on at all that passed as if we had been spectators of a *festa*. It was impossible to fire, for had we done so, we should have killed more of our own people than of the enemy." Another eyewitness, Francesco Gonzaga, declared that the sight from the battlements would have moved "a stone to compassion." A Venetian envoy sent home a report declaring that "Hell has nothing to compare with the present state of Rome." The only ray of hope amid the evident mayhem was that the forces of the Italian League would come to the rescue. Order had broken down so completely among the imperial troops after the death of their own commander that they could easily have been driven from the city had the pope's allies moved boldly. They did not, however, and earned everlasting scorn from the great contemporary poet Ariosto for their cowardice:

> In every part you see how Rome is woe,
> Mid ruthless rapine, murder, fire, and rape.
> See all to wasting rack and ruin go,
> And nothing human or divine escape.
> The league's men hear the shrieks, behold the glow
> Of hostile fires, and lo! they backward shape
> Their course, where they should hurry on their way,
> And leave the pontiff to his foes a prey.
>
> (*Orlando Furioso* XXXIII, 55)[2]

When the Germans and Spaniards later occupied the castle, one of their leaders frankly noted that the Church leaders were confined "in a narrow chamber," and even that "They were making a great lamentation and weeping bitterly; as for us, we all became rich."[3]

The Spectacle of Benvenuto Cellini

Some of the inmates of the castle during the siege may themselves have been more than a little hard to take. For instance, the famous scalawag and artist Benvenuto Cellini helped in the defense of the castle in 1527 — and if his self-serving *Autobiography* is to be believed, he was one of the staunchest fighters. We can only imagine the effect that the presence of this mercurial and egotistical figure had on the soldiers and Church leaders contemplating the destruction of their city. It's a safe bet that in his relentless boasting he did not calm things down. His account of this period in the autobiography begins with the claim — not impossible but highly improbable — that he took a group of men to see the advancing imperial troops and, after they had fired arquebuses, they witnessed "the most extraordinary uproar arise among the enemy, because one of our shots had killed [the duke of] Borbone." As if the death of the enemy commander was not a great enough achievement, Cellini also claims to have taken charge of the cannons at Castel Sant'Angelo "and with them I killed many of the enemy's men; and if I had not done so, the part of the invading army that had entered Rome that morning would have come directly to the Castello.... Through boldness I forced myself to do what was impossible; enough to say I was the reason why the Castello was saved that morning and that those other artillerymen went back to fulfill their duties."[4] The true military heroes of this siege — the Swiss, who had lost so many men, prominently among them — must have gritted their teeth reading all this, and Cellini's modest addition, "if I recounted in any detail the daring deeds I performed in that cruel, hellish place, I would amaze the world."

Among these are his plot to bombard a meeting of the imperial leadership that would have effectively decapitated the opposing force. But he was stopped by Church officials, he claims, who argued they would then have no one to negotiate with. Perhaps the only realistic detail in this whole bizarre account was this:

"When night fell and the enemy entered Rome, we in the Castello, and most particularly myself, who has always delighted in seeing new things, stood there contemplating this unbelievable spectacle and conflagration, which was of a magnitude that those who were situated in any other spot but the Castello could neither see nor imagine."[5] This probably does fairly capture the astonishment of all barricaded in the Castel Sant'Angelo on that Roman spring evening, though some may have been equally astonished by the flamboyance of Cellini.

Imperial Fury Unleashed

Nor were the besieged entirely out of harm's way. Two guard towers at the opposite end of the bridge leading to the castle had been taken over by imperial forces, and soldiers skilled in the use of crossbows were able to shoot anyone who showed himself too openly on the ramparts.

But this was nothing compared to the slaughter that ensued in the rest of the city. The imperial forces had paid dearly to breach the city wall. Not only had the duke of Bourbon been killed, but the commander Gian d'Urbina received a facial wound from a pike wielded by a Swiss guard. He and his entire army turned to bestial fury, killing virtually every person they came upon until they realized that it might be profitable to capture some for ransom. Cardinal Ponzetti, an eighty-year-old, died from mistreatment. The brilliant theologian Cardinal Cajetan was also tortured, but survived. Others were interrogated — brutally and slowly — for information about hidden loot (some died, others killed themselves).

Ordinary human decency simply disappeared. All the patients of the Hospital of Santo Spirito were killed, as were the children of the Pietà orphanage. The same occurred at other places of healing and charity throughout the city. Diplomatic immunities were disregarded: embassies, usually sacrosanct, were ransacked as blithely as churches. Even palaces of known imperialists such as the Colonna were a target. Convents were invaded and nuns raped and then often sold into prostitution, as were many of the city's female nobility. Lutheran soldiers killed an old priest for refusing to give the Eucharist to a donkey. Five hundred men were killed at the main altar of St. Peter's, tombs were violated, relics desecrated, the basilica itself was turned into a stable, as was the Sistine Chapel. Probably no outrage committed in war up until that time failed to occur during the imperial sack of Rome. Contemporaries commented that even the Turks had never done such things.

The immediate destruction was terrible, and it had long-term effects on the city. Within the year the population was half of what it had been before the invasion. No one can say for certain how many Romans died, but ten to twenty thousand is a safe estimate. Some died immediately of violence, others slowly starved or succumbed to the plague that began as a result of bodies left to rot in piles in the streets. The air was so foul that, when the wind blew the wrong way, even the inmates at the castle could not go out on the high parapets. Foreigners, Spaniards (a large contingent at least since the time of the Borgias), and Germans in particular believed they would never be safe among the remaining Romans again and went elsewhere. The accumulated wealth and art of the city had been mostly defaced or simply stolen. Whole libraries had disappeared. Fortunately, the Vatican Library had been spared because of strong intervention by the imperial commanders, but the papal archives suffered serious damage. The Holy See was able to buy back many lost items over the next two decades; some were never accounted for. Rome lost many of the scholars, artists, and humanists who had helped make it such a splendid prize when they fled to their places of origin or other centers of culture and feared to return to Rome.

The sack had evil effects on the imperial forces, too. As had been expected, the breakdown in discipline that accompanied the looting spilled over to internal discipline as well. Officers began to fear their own men. Food shortages became acute among the

Siege, Dissolution, Rebirth 85

soldiers since the normal means of provisioning the city had been disrupted and the forces of the Italian League, though too fearful to attempt rescuing the pope, blocked several of the usual paths for shipping food. Wine and water both were scarce. Virtually anything flammable was used for cooking or heating. Fights broke out between the German soldiers and the Spaniards over booty and mere necessities, which often led to murder. The bodies left rotting in the open sun began to infect the invaders, too. More than two thousand Germans died of the plague within two months of the invasion.

A Spanish eyewitness described the conditions of natives and invaders alike:

> In Rome, the chief city of Christendom, no bells ring, no churches are open, no Masses are said, Sundays and feast-days have ceased. The rich shops of the merchants are turned into stables; the most splendid palaces are stripped bare; many houses are burnt to the ground; in others the doors and windows are broken and carried away; the streets are changed into dunghills. The stench of dead bodies is terrible; men and beasts have a common grave, and in the churches I have seen corpses that dogs have gnawed. In the public places tables are set close together at which piles of ducats are gambled for. The air rings with blasphemies fit to make good men, if such there be, wish that they were deaf. I know nothing wherewith I can compare it except it be the destruction of Jerusalem.[6]

There were few good things to come out of the 1527 sack of Rome. One, however, involved a kind of reconciliation between Clement and Pompeio Colonna, bitter enemies but united in their love for the city. The fate of Rome at the hands of the invaders quelled their previous animosities toward each other. They met in the castle on the first day of June 1527 and, tears in their eyes, agreed to seek some solution that would prevent further damage to the city. Colonna was very vigorous in pursuing that aim and received back from the pope all the honors and offices — along with others — he had lost because of his participation in the uprising. In fact, mostly thanks to Colonna's good offices, within a few days an agreement acceptable to all parties was struck. The pope had to agree to pay a ransom of four hundred thousand ducats and give up several cities in the states controlled by the Church as well as Castel Sant'Angelo. It was a heavy price, so heavy that, in fact, Clement was never able fully to pay it. This arrangement would soon lead to further humiliations of the pope.

Damage to Charles V's Reputation

The sack was not even good for the emperor Charles V. Though he at first took pleasure in the victory, the reports that followed quickly convinced him that the whole episode could only damage his reputation. He had been ambiguous in his attitude toward looting by imperial forces all during the Italian campaign. Like many rulers of the day, he was forced by circumstances to allow the soldiers he had recruited (with implied possibilities for war booty) to take what they needed for immediate survival. Everyone anticipated that there would also be some additional benefit when wealthy cities were taken. But the unprecedented barbarity at Rome reflected quite badly on Charles, and not only among his rivals in France and England. The Spanish cardinals and bishops reproached him for letting such a sacrilege occur. Ludwig Pastor, the greatest historian of the papacy, summarized Charles's problems in this way: "The spectacle of the army of the secular head of Christendom, the protector of the Church, carrying murder, fire, and outrage into the city of its spiritual head, was turned to account to the fullest extent. Even in the heart of Charles's empire, in Spain, a by no means inconsiderable opposition was raised to a policy which had ended at last in turning him into the jailer of the Pope."[7]

Conditions were so bad that Charles even had difficulty in appointing a replacement for his slain commander, the duke of

Bourbon. He tried the duke of Ferrara, who declined to become the head of "a gang of mutineers." The result was that from the invasion in May until near the end of 1527 there simply was no supreme commander of the imperial forces. As the material available for robbery and amusement was reduced, the emperor's army began to shrink from disease and desertion. Even the negotiations with the pope seemed to have been erratic. It is no wonder that Charles V, in theory the heir of the Roman emperors and leader of all Christendom as Holy Roman Emperor, offered an apology for what his troops, without his explicit instructions, had done to the pope and to Rome. He even stated that he would have preferred not to have won the battle for Rome in the way that it had happened.

The Disbanding of the Swiss Guard

In the meantime, it appears that one of the conditions of the deal between the emperor and the pope was that Clement give up his Swiss guards. According to one source, the remaining Swiss forces were made to leave the castle with all their goods and belongings[8] — not very much, since they had taken refuge in the castle and their quarters in the Vatican had been ransacked by imperial troops. Even worse than this melancholy retreat was the fact that the Swiss were replaced by Spanish and German bodyguards — their bitter rivals among mercenaries of the time. The pope could not do much under the circumstances, but he must have felt some guilt over the arrangements he had made for his own situation since he recognized responsibility for the Swiss survivors and tried to get permission for them to join the new guards. Twelve Swiss accepted the offer, including a few officers. Herkules Göldli, who had commanded the surviving Swiss after the death of Gaspar Röist in their defense of the retreating pope, declined and left Rome.

It is not clear that all the remaining Swiss guards did so as well, though it is possible they also returned to Switzerland. Over the following six or seven years — until Clement's death in 1534 — various numbers of Swiss, from a few dozen to almost ninety at a time, show up in the Vatican archives as guards of the Apostolic Palace. Since this was one of the services the Swiss performed prior to the sack of Rome, some may have turned to that task rather than submit to being under the command of German officers, an uncomfortable position since the Germans were primarily Lutherans without much use for the pope or his allies, to say the least. Other Swiss may have been newly recruited to participate in this corps of men who did not have the same type of military responsibilities as the papal bodyguards proper, but still must have had much to do since the entire city for some time after its sack suffered from the breakdown of order.

In fact, only two weeks after the initial mayhem in Rome, the Spanish and German soldiers of the imperial army, impatient for the pay they were still being denied, left Rome, plundered the Umbrian city of Narni about fifty miles to the north, then returned and inflicted a new round of horrors on the Holy City. By the end of the year, since ransom still had not been paid, the imperial troops went on another rampage, this time in the area outside of Rome known as the Campagna, and upon returning to Rome "threatened to hang their captains and cut the Pope to pieces if they did not receive their arrears of pay,"[9] a real possibility now that the pope was being "guarded" by forces with no real interest in his safety. Ludwig Pastor, summarizing the extant sources, reports that Spaniards, the most vicious among the invaders, stood guard over the papal bedchamber, and overall "within the narrow confines of the castle, kept under closest watch by a fierce soldiery, [the pope] spent his days as in a 'living tomb.'"[10] The German and Spanish soldiers, it seems clear, would have swiftly carried off the pope for ransom, whatever negotiations were under way, had the emperor not taken a strong hand in preventing this further outrage by his own troops.

On December 7, 1527, almost exactly seven months after fleeing to Castel Sant'Angelo, Pope Clement VII adopted a dangerous ruse as a last-ditch effort to save himself: he secretly stole out of the castle disguised as a peasant carrying a basket and an empty sack. He fled to Orvieto, a small medieval city north of Rome, where, by an odd coincidence, the English ambassador sent by Henry VIII to procure his divorce from Catherine of Aragon met him. The ambassador soon reported back to England on Clement's sorry state. Somehow about 150 men from Clement's German-Swiss bodyguard were able to join him there, where he could be seen out walking with eight mounted knights and thirty foot soldiers watching over him. Clement was not able to return to Rome until February 11, 1528. When he did, he found a city, once the jewel of Renaissance Europe, utterly devastated. Frail and in increasingly poor health, he grew a long beard — unusual for the time — as a sign of mourning for all the death and destruction. On top of everything, he had to come to terms with the emperor Charles V. They signed an agreement, and when Clement went to Bologna in 1530 to crown Charles formally as the Holy Roman Emperor, his guards were present in the Cathedral of St. Petronius standing in two rows and wearing shining armor.[11] All of this pomp and circumstance must have been small consolation to the pope and his entourage compared with the ruin of the fortunes of the papacy and the Holy City.

Silence about the Sack in Switzerland

Even in Switzerland, there was little comfort. The divisions introduced by the Reformation at Zurich and the perception that the Swiss guards had stubbornly insisted on remaining with the pope of Rome against the orders of Swiss authorities combined to produce a kind of silence about the slain and the survivors. There was certainly no cult of heroism associated with them in newly Protestant Switzerland. Commandant Röist's widow tried to keep the memory alive. But it was a hopeless task. Later, when the Swiss guards would be reconstituted, Zurich would no longer be the main place of recruitment or the home of the commandant. The center of recruitment and command would pass to Lucerne and the other Catholic regions of the country. In Rome, the heroic last hours of the guards were held in high esteem and kept in memory. Some of the figures associated with the earlier formation and staffing of the Swiss Guard kept the issue of restoring the Guard to its original status and configuration before Clement. The pope died, however, before circumstances had sufficiently changed for restoration to become a real possibility.

Clement's successor, Paul III (Alessandro Farnese), was a transitional figure. The scion of a noble and wealthy Roman family, he still had one foot in the Renaissance papacy, the other in the new currents in the Church that would lead to the austere Catholic Counter-Reformation. He was cautious by nature, a trait further accented by the uncertain time in which he was elected pope. Ever since his election in 1534, Paul III had been sympathetic to the idea of reestablishing the Swiss Guard, but unwilling to commit himself to act. In June 1537, after some arm-twisting by Cardinal Filonardi, the pope gave the cardinal a commission to recruit five hundred Swiss from the Catholic areas of Switzerland — for the purpose of repelling the attacks of the Turks. There was as yet no real enthusiasm in Switzerland for reconstituting the Guard. Several requests in Swiss towns met with stiff resistance, not least because the Holy See still owed back pay to former guards and their families. Filonardi and Cardinal Ardinghelli kept constant pressure on Paul III, explaining to him that he could use the Germans against the Turks; the Swiss were best for his own bodyguard. And a close connection to Switzerland — a formidable military power — would help deter other nations from pressuring the Holy See again.

With Filonardi's advice, Paul III appointed the knights Girolamo Franco and Albert Rosin to begin the process of reconstituting the historic Guard. They met with anti-papal opposition in Switzerland, however, and decided that it would be best to recruit a papal guard for Bologna first, as a prelude to the harder task of recruiting for Rome.[12] In January of 1542, 150 Swiss set out over the Alps for Italy under the leadership of Josue von Beroldingen of Uri. They were received warmly at Bologna in April, and were assured that both they and their homeland were held in fatherly esteem by the pope. It probably brought no little satisfaction to the Swiss that they were replacing a German contingent, who had been dismissed to make room for them. It would take another six years — until 1548 — before the Swiss guards would take up similar duties again in the Holy City.

Two things seemed to be needed before the reconstitution of the Guard would become possible. Or perhaps it would be better to say that one development had to occur — in two places. Basically, the remaining nightmares from the sack of Rome had to be overcome both in the Holy See and in Switzerland before Rome could be truly Rome again. At Rome, the process began because of a consummate work of art, Michelangelo's *Last Judgment*. Clement VII had invited the great Florentine back to Rome after the imperial troops departed and agreed with him about the subject of the frescoes to be done behind the altar in the Sistine Chapel. The work — which was to reflect the agonies of the whole city of Rome during Clement's papacy — was not begun until the time of Paul III. On the vigil of All Saints' Day in 1541 this volcanic creation was unveiled. Many religious people thought the nudes more appropriate to a tavern than the chapel of the Supreme Pontiff. For Paul III, however, it produced a kind of catharsis in representing the torments that many painfully remembered.[13]

By 1546, when the German governor of Milan assassinated the duke of Piacenza, Paul III was ready for a complete change. He declared his desire that the Germans leave his service in Rome and a purely Swiss corps replace them.[14] Perhaps providentially, Nikolaus von Meggen was in Rome shortly thereafter and discussed the reconstruction of the guards with the pope and several cardinals. It appears the churchmen decided that von Meggen would be a good candidate for Swiss commandant; however, because he was mayor of Lucerne, it was impossible for him to move to Rome. He suggested instead a relative known to the papal Curia, his nephew Jost von Meggen, a highly accomplished man and distinguished humanist with much experience of Europe and even of several places in the Middle East. The pope agreed and wrote to the Lucerne council requesting that they select and send him their best warriors who were distinguished for their fidelity to the ancient Catholic faith, for courage, and for loyalty to the Holy See.[15]

Renewed Spirit in Switzerland

In Switzerland, the healing process was hastened by the good relationships between the papal officials and the Swiss forces established in Bologna. As word of this happy collaboration was carried home to Switzerland, enthusiasm grew, at least in Catholic areas, for a new papal service, even though mercenary tours remained illegal. The papal recruiters found it easy to enlist a full complement for the papal force. Negotiations about the re-creation of the guards at Rome caused complex reactions in early 1548. Within the Swiss confederation, certain areas were strongly in favor of the Guard, others naturally opposed. Some feared the loss of so many good men for Switzerland itself and the potential for conflict with the emperor. Others objected to what appeared to be the transfer of authority to Lucerne above the other Catholic regions. Yet a strong civility marked these discussions, and problems were worked out through wide consultation. When the emperor raised no objection to the replacement of his German guards by the Swiss, the Catholic cantons declared on February 13, 1548, that the way was clear for the turnover to take place.[16] Appointment of officers was left in the hands of the commander, and the pope communicated his desire that the guards set out quickly for Rome.

When the Catholics sent out a recruitment letter — even to the Protestant regions of Zurich and Bern — it was received with respect. Not surprisingly, the areas most committed to the Reformation declined the offer. The strongly Catholic cantons such as Appenzell and Fribourg responded with far more enthusiasm, but even they had some questions about pay and other practical matters. More seriously, they wanted to know what the guards would be used for. In spite of everything, the man agreed upon as the new commander, Jost von Meggen, had no trouble assembling the names of two hundred men for the papal guard, as well as an additional twenty-five "volunteers" from influential families whom he could not refuse, some of whom would later prove quite unsuitable for the specific kinds of duties they had to perform.[17]

The contract of the new corps of guards with the Holy See was essentially the same as the one that Clement VII had worked out with his own Swiss guards years earlier. It covered many specific details such as pay and expenses for service in Rome, bonuses during the pope's trips around Italy, food and other provisions while traveling or should war break out, expenses during convalescence, pensions, and compensation if a guard was dismissed. The Swiss also committed themselves to the pope for his whole life, a new provision since the Germans who had just left only agreed to two-year tours of duty at a time. Von Meggen shrewdly negotiated a limit of two hundred guards with the pope's representatives, a number that gave him the freedom to get rid of guards he did not want without angering important figures at home. In mid-February 1548, officers and men began to gather in the town of Altdorf in the canton of Uri in inner Switzerland.

They departed for Rome on February 17, even though the weather and the season were not the best for such a voyage. Passing through Lugano and Milan, the troops arrived in Rome on a date that has not been recorded, but seems to have been sometime around the beginning or middle of March — a quick passage over the Alps in winter. Things seem to have gone quite smoothly under von Meggen's leadership in the first months in Rome. The Germans departed without incident, and the Swiss again took up their old barracks near the Apostolic Palace. After a nearly twenty-one-year hiatus following the military disaster on May 6, 1527, the papal Swiss guards had returned to their old service, a bit warier perhaps after their experience with international intrigue over Rome and the papacy, but on much the same terms as they had left it.

Commandant Jost von Meggen

Jost von Meggen (1509–59) was born into one of the most distinguished Lucerne families and received, under his father's careful guidance, the best upbringing and education available in the city at that time. He studied first in Lucerne, where his father served as mayor, with Oswald Myconius, a friend of both the internationally acclaimed Dutch humanist Erasmus of Rotterdam and the painter Hans Holbein, and a follower of Huldrych Zwingli and the Protestant Reformation. Though the young man would also come to know several more of the most prominent leaders of the Reformation, he was not drawn into its orbit. He spent three years under the tutelage of Heinrich Loriti ("Gloreanus"), a famous humanist from Basel, who oversaw his remarkable progress in classical languages as well as ancient history and geography. Von Meggen was also fascinated by modern languages (he was later reputed to speak nine of them) and the contemporary world, and lost no time in pursuing studies abroad as well. In 1525, at only sixteen, he spent time studying French in Orléans and became familiar with the very best manners of the day. In his early twenties, he had already been named a member of the Lucerne city council and served in other important political posts around Switzerland.

Von Meggen had a restless and inquiring mind and was not fully satisfied by his public offices. In 1542, he left his wife and father at home to undertake a journey to the Holy Land. Passing through Italy and Greece, he eventually reached Jerusalem, where he visited the sacred sites, using the Bible as a guidebook. The tomb of Jesus made a special impression on him. On the return journey, a fierce storm blew his ship off course to Egypt and kept it there for some time. He took advantage of the opportunity and saw that country's antiquities as well as Mount Sinai. When the winds were more favorable, he sailed to Italy and made a brief stop in Rome, where he was well received by the Swiss then serving in the mixed German-Swiss papal guard. It is likely that this highly cultivated son of a distinguished Swiss figure also began to make various other acquaintances in the Holy City at that time.

It was only natural then, given his accomplishments and experience, that the Catholic cantons of Switzerland sent him on a special and confidential mission to Rome in 1547. He seems to have made an impression on several cardinals and been received favorably by the pope himself, because he was already known and immediately accepted among the Curia when his name was proposed by his uncle as a possible commandant for the reconstituted Swiss Guard. Typical for a man of Jost's strong humanistic interests in that period, he took advantage of his time in Rome to familiarize himself with the sites and remains of the ancient world that had begun to be uncovered and studied by Renaissance scholars and artists. He was a man well suited to diplomatic and cultural circles, but was he a man to lead a military detachment?

He had theoretical knowledge of military matters; his post in Switzerland had brought him into contact with such questions. But he had never served in the field. Nevertheless, he established a reputation for himself from the very first as accepting nothing less than exemplary performance by the guards. Unsuitable guards, hastily recruited when the possibility of reconstituting the old force opened up in both Rome and Switzerland, were summarily sent home. Most of those rejected would not accept strict discipline. A few proved dishonest. In one case, Heiny Wiesenmeyer of Willisau stabbed another guard named Hochstocker from Zug. Hochstocker died and Wiesenmeyer tried to cast suspicion on

Spanish soldiers. Von Meggen was not the kind of humanist who was paralyzed in the face of real evils. These and other problems were dealt with swiftly and only served to raise the general confidence in his leadership.[18] He had not been able to control every detail of recruiting in Switzerland, but in Rome things ran according to the commandant's high standards.

Von Meggen wisely went back to the structure that had served the guards well in their earlier incarnation. Officers and enlisted men were sorted into the same general pattern, though he divided the men into "watches" named after their Swiss cantons of origin: Lucerne, Uri, Unterwalden, Zug, Glarus, and Solothurn. Later, these became generic names for tasks to be done and might be carried out by men from several different regions.[19] Recruiting, outfitting, and equipping these men — two hundred in total — was expensive for the Holy See. Even so, pay was not great. Guards had difficulties keeping up with the cost of living, let alone saving something for the future. Von Meggen petitioned both the Holy Father and Switzerland for some relief in the circumstance, and adjustments were forthcoming. The Swiss guards especially appreciated — and made liberal use of — the papal exemption that allowed them to buy Roman wine tax-free. Essentially, the Swiss sought to return to the level of compensation and service they had enjoyed when they were interrupted by the 1527 sack of the city.

Paul III died on November 10, 1549, a little over a year and a half after the refounding of the guards. He had given von Meggen explicit instructions about what to do both as he neared death and after. One thing that, as in the past, was quite important was to maintain order around the Vatican in the interim. Von Meggen and his men patrolled in full armor at the entrances to the Apostolic Palace. Other troops occupied the neighborhoods more distant from the Vatican proper. A few problems arose, but by careful planning the usual public disorders were happily prevented.

Two Reforming Popes

Paul's successor, Julius III (Giovanni Maria del Monte), was also a serious reformer. Del Monte had served as the presiding legate at the Council of Trent, the major Catholic reform event in the sixteenth century, long promised and finally inaugurated by Paul III, which sought not only to deal with the Protestant divisions from the Church but to implement those difficult changes in structures and attitudes that were needed inside the Church, perhaps nowhere more so than in Rome. Julius kept the council moving, even when external events of a political nature made some of its main tasks impossible. He seems to have wished to "reform" the guards as well, primarily by cutting the force by fifty men.

This reduction in force did not sit well with von Meggen, his men, or their friends in the Roman Curia. It is difficult to say whether the proposal was a cost-cutting effort on Julius's part or perhaps the result of the pope's intuition that the papacy was moving, as it indeed was, toward a different model than it had followed in the recent past. There would be no more corrupt Renaissance prince popes like Alexander VI, or warriors such as Julius II, or high-living epicures like Leo X. As the papacy and the whole Roman Church began to change character, it would have only been natural to think that the guards, too, should undergo some restructuring. Von Meggen threatened that the pope might have to find another commander if the restructuring involved the loss of fifty halberdiers, the lowest level soldiers who performed the majority of the tasks that needed doing. In any event, Julius III and his staff agreed not to make the change unless their coffers were empty or other troops were dismissed first.

When Julius passed from the scene, he was replaced (after the brief two-week papacy of Marcellus II), by Paul IV, one of the great and little-known reforming popes of the sixteenth century. A historian of the period says of him: "If Rome — papal Rome — bears today, and has borne for centuries, something of the appearance of a monastery, if the modern popes, whatever their faults as individuals and as popes, have all lived, primarily, as priests, in a setting of prayer and a certain religious decorum, this restoration of what should be is due, in the largest possible measure, to Paul IV." And he adds:

> Through him, at last, the Paganism of the Renaissance is driven from the papacy, the last association of secularism with that high office broken. His elemental zeal, his fire, his whole-hearted surrender of inexhaustible energy to the purpose in hand, his contempt for compromise and half measures, his entire devotion to the one purpose of purifying the Church and making it once more the fit instrument of God's service...found the fulness of opportunity.[20]

It is no surprise to find that this kind of man was equally decisive in his relations with the Swiss. This pope immediately showed his appreciation for the guards — even spending a long time in formal conversation with the Swiss commander about various matters — and invited von Meggen always to bring any requests to his personal attention. Unlike his predecessors, Paul IV paid the guards on time and in the amounts the agreements with them specified. He even took the initiative to put his own stamp on the guards by ordering them to be given new red-and-white uniforms. The pope was a monkish man; he had founded, along with Cardinal Cajetan, the new order of Theatines, a strict and energetically pious group. He often ignored traditional arrangements in the Curia and in political relationships in pursuing his reforms. At the same time, he also knew the value of what was sound in the situation he inherited. It is clear that his wooing of von Meggen represented both his appreciation for the Swiss guards in themselves and his hopes that the Swiss would help him in his struggles with the emperor, France, England, and the Turks — and in the handling of some of their supporters at the Roman court.

Von Meggen as Diplomat

By this point, von Meggen had served under four popes, and his experience in Rome made him a valuable source of information at home in Switzerland. He carried on a lively correspondence with Swiss authorities on matters relating both to large political questions, with which Rome was inevitably involved, as well as matters relating more closely to the Catholic faith. Because of the denominational divisions in Switzerland, the Catholic cantons especially valued their relationship with the Holy See as one way of maintaining their identity. As the Catholic Counter-Reformation proceeded, those regions decided that they needed a kind of permanent representative in the Roman Curia. Von Meggen was the natural choice for this task, which he carried out faithfully and zealously.[21] The pope seems to have appreciated his work as well. Toward the end of von Meggen's life he was awarded honorary Roman citizenship by the "Senate and the People of Rome," the ancient imperial formula SPQR.

Jost von Meggen was arguably the perfect commandant of the guards at this moment in the history of the Catholic Church. The times called for less of an outright military stance on the part of the Swiss and more of a nuanced combination of diplomacy and order. Von Meggen traveled several times between Rome and Switzerland on various missions, papal and personal, during his last years. His health started to fail, and neither place seemed to offer much relief. Clearly, he sensed that the end was drawing near, because he had a tomb prepared in the German cemetery of the Vatican. He would never use it, however. Despite his growing weakness, von Meggen had to travel to Lucerne in the winter of 1558 to deal with family business. The rigors of the journey exhausted him, and he died on March 17, 1559, just a few months before Paul IV. He was buried in St. Peter's Church in Lucerne with many honors. Though he was the first commander of the Swiss Guard to die in bed of natural causes rather than in battle, he ended his life away from the city he had served in for many years. With his death and the pope's, the Church and the Swiss Guard moved out of the turmoil of the Renaissance and early Reformation and into the full age of the Catholic Reform.

Left: Helmets in the Armory.

Below: Guard duty at Sant'Anna Gate.

Cardinal Matthew Schiner and Swiss guards (Painting in the Mess Hall of the guards).

The guards in eighteenth-century uniforms.

The guards in 1906 celebrating their four-hundredth anniversary.

Left: Commandant Elmar Th. Mäder in dress uniform.

Right: Guard duty at the Arch of Bells.

Below: The swearing in of a new guard.

Above: Swiss bodyguards accompany John Paul II's body to St. Peter's Basilica.

Right: The Guard band and flag.

Right: Plainclothes guards at the Wednesday audience.

Below: The guards with Benedict XVI.

Chapter Five

Years of Peace — and Napoleonic War

AFTER A HALF CENTURY of battles and turmoil, the papacy and the Swiss Guard entered into a period of relative peace toward the end of the sixteenth century. The popes did fight some painful wars: in 1557 Paul IV decided to mount a resistance to Spanish designs in Italy at Paliano (where a Swiss army he had recruited lost several hundred men), and in 1571 a Christian fleet defeated the Turks in the naval battle of Lepanto. But these were the prelude to a much more tranquil period for everyone concerned until relatively modern times. Yet the period also had its tensions, particularly at the beginning, when the Catholic Counter-Reformation was clearly formulated and given fresh movement by the Council of Trent. In Switzerland, the divisions between Catholic and Protestant cantons could not help but generate various problems. Rival nations such as France and Spain allied with and played cantons off against one another, their political interests taking precedence often enough over religious alignments. At the same time, everyone had a vested interest in making sure that Switzerland did not become chaotic or that its soldiers did not become unavailable for foreign service because of problems at home.

For the Holy See, there were three important goals to be reached in Switzerland: implementing the Council of Trent, harnessing the intellectual energy of the Jesuits in the Catholic cantons of Lucerne and Fribourg, and establishing a permanent nunciature, a kind of papal embassy, among the Swiss.[1] Since the commandant of the Swiss Guard often functioned as a kind of ambassador to the Holy See during these years (sometimes officially so), it was only natural that he would also help with diplomatic movement in the opposite direction, especially in the pope's dealings with Catholic cantons. But he participated in dealings with the newly Protestant areas as well. The Swiss commandant was even used in relations with other Italian cities, and with good reason since Swiss papal guards were stationed around Italy. In 1550, contingents of 125 Swiss soldiers each were committed to protect papal legations at Bologna and Ravenna by the Catholic cantons. Schwyz, Unterwalden, and Uri in 1560 provided a fifty-man garrison at Ancona, an important Italian port facing east; eight years later, Zug designated fifty men to guard the pope's cardinal legate at Ferrara.[2]

One indication of the tensions that existed at the time may be glimpsed in the treaty between the Holy See and the Catholic cantons. In early 1562, the Swiss were able for the first time to send delegates to the Council of Trent, the great reforming event for the Catholic Church. The council had begun to be held intermittently in 1545 and concluded in 1563, so the Swiss were absent during most of its deliberations. Their greatest worry in the years after the council ended was resistance and criticism — and possibly direct attacks — from the Protestant cantons as they went about implementing the conciliar reforms. As a result, the Catholic Swiss sent a legate, Hans Zumbrunnen, to the pope to negotiate a mutual aid pact. In 1565, Pope Pius IV (Giovanni Angelo Medici) pledged twenty thousand crowns to the Catholics if they were attacked, along with a thousand Italian arquebusiers to be paid by the Holy See, in addition to other guarantees. The Swiss, in turn, promised six thousand troops if the pope was attacked. The pope agreed, further, that only native-born Swiss would be admitted to his guards, and the commandant would be an officer from Lucerne, as the most prominent Catholic canton.[3]

The pope's immediate successors did not always live up to every detail of these arrangements, but Lucerne did become central to the administration of the Guard: from 1592 until 1878 every commandant came from that Catholic city.

Pius IV died in the same year that he signed the treaty. His successor, Pius V, a pious monk, sought to implement the new principles generated at Trent. Shortly after Pius's election in January of 1566, Lucerne named Jost Segesser of Brunegg as guard commandant. Segesser had been, along with his brother Albrecht, a ward of an earlier commandant, Jost von Meggen, and they had been expected after von Meggen's death to share the command of their stepfather. Because of other influences in the papal court, however, Pius IV had decided in 1559 to appoint Kaspar Leo von Silenen instead. Von Silenen was an experienced soldier and the son of Kaspar von Silenen, the first commandant of the Guard, who had died in the battle of Rimini serving Pope Leo X.[4] But in spite of this distinguished background, his appointment ruffled several feathers. The mayor and Diet in Lucerne had recommended the two Segesser brothers, as had their esteemed stepfather. So Switzerland was not happy about the pope's choice. In Rome, the situation was no better: the officers and men of the Roman guards had been looking forward to the brothers' continuing in their stepfather's good ways. Naturally, the pope's preferment of von Silenen also angered the brothers, who announced they would no longer serve in Rome and departed to take over the command of the Swiss guards in the papal territory of Ravenna in northeastern Italy.

Kaspar Leo von Silenen's Command

The new commandant had already served as an officer in the Guard. And he had fought, and been taken captive, after being wounded, at the disastrous battle of Paliano. Rumors circulated that he had handled himself poorly during the fighting and was responsible for the loss of an ensign and Swiss standard, but these stories seem to have been started by rivals. His comrades from Paliano testified to his bravery. Furthermore, von Silenen worked to reassemble the survivors of his company in Rome afterward. In fact, it seems he was the victim of bad behavior rather than the perpetrator. When he used connections to get a relative, Baptist Feer, an appointment to study in Rome, Feer not only proved too lazy to take advantage of the opportunity, but also he had an affair with von Silenen's wife while he was traveling on business. It is a sign of von Silenen's character that he would not allow the usual penalty — the death sentence — to be applied against his relative, and his wife was merely sent to a cloistered convent. In spite of these events and other attempts to smear him, von Silenen was appointed commandant of the Swiss guards in Ravenna in February of 1559, so it appears that the pope and the papal Curia had a quite high opinion of von Silenen.

That reading of the situation is confirmed by the fact that only three months later the pope recalled him to Rome to become commandant of his personal bodyguards. Von Silenen's appointment over the Segesser brothers may have been a diplomatic compromise. The position of commandant of the Swiss Guard was always highly coveted, and during von Silenen's absence there had been serious attempts to appoint an Italian in his former place as a lieutenant, which might have put the newcomer in line for something even higher. The Swiss guards made objections to the Diet in Lucerne as well as to the pope. They stated in no uncertain terms that they wanted no foreign officers imposed on them. The pope's unexpected appointment of von Silenen in Rome may have been a subtle way to respect the wishes of the rank and file that command remain in Swiss hands, but it was not complete acquiescence.

In any event, von Silenen assumed control of the guards and, after some initial resistance, put the command in order. He had just begun a vacation back home in Altdorf in the summer of 1559 when word arrived of the death of Pope Paul IV. Since the guards are an integral part of the conclave when a new pope is elected, he returned to Rome immediately to oversee preparations. It was a long and bitterly divided election process, and von Silenen reported back to the Swiss authorities on the various factions in conflict who kept agreement from being reached until Christmas — one of the longest conclaves in the history of the Catholic Church. Giovanni Angelo Medici emerged from the conclave as pope and took the name of Pius IV. In the most florid and elaborate language, he immediately assured the Swiss in Rome and back in the homeland of his deep gratitude for their support and of his intention to continue respecting the agreements that his predecessors had made with them.

But Pius IV wanted more out of the relationship, and it soon showed. First, he had von Silenen arrest Cardinal Carlo Carafa, who had been one of the commandant's greatest patrons, and the cardinal's nephew Alfonso. Naturally, von Silenen did not want to do this, but all things considered, he had no choice. Both were taken to Castel Sant'Angelo, where they were held under guard as enemies of the pope. Pius then requested four thousand to six thousand Swiss troops, on the pretext that he feared the French Huguenots were planning to take over Avignon, a French city historically controlled by the papacy. The Turks, he argued, were also threatening in the East. Back in Switzerland, this request was met with various evasions. The popes had a tendency to seek Swiss soldiers for their immediate needs, but to put off payment. The new pope and his predecessor had dithered over twenty thousand crowns still promised the Swiss, which they wanted deposited somewhere outside of Rome as a sign of good faith. Negotiations opened for a new pact to work out these issues, but they dragged on and, in July of 1564, before they could come to a conclusion, Kaspar Leo von Silenen died.

The pope used this occasion to exert greater pressure on the Swiss. Without consulting anyone, he appointed his cousin Gabriele Serbelloni, an Italian, commandant of the Swiss Guard.[5] All the Swiss were deeply upset by this move, but it had the good effect of bringing both sides to an agreement. The pope promised, as mentioned above, to deposit money in a Milanese bank as a sign of good faith, and to allow only citizens of Lucerne to be the Swiss commandant in Rome. Furthermore, from then on, only native-born Swiss would be allowed to serve as papal guards. While these specifics were being worked out, however, six months passed and the pope himself died. His funeral was presided over by a company of guards without a commandant. Pius V quickly remedied this by appointing a certain Wilhelm Henneberg, who had been made an interim lieutenant. But shortly after, a Latin note in the papal archives reports that he had been replaced by *Jodicus Sexer,* in German none other than Jost Segesser, who had seemed to have left the Roman scene forever.

The Talented Jost Segesser

Jost Segesser would preside over the guards for more than two and a half decades (1566–92), and by the time of his death his post and the men he commanded underwent a deep change. There is no secret as to why he made a sudden reappearance. Both of the mayors of Lucerne, Nikolaus Amlehn and Jost Pfyffer, along with other prominent men of that city, recommended him in the warmest terms to the Holy See.[6] Things had changed enough in Rome that, whatever political intrigues had kept Jost and his brother from command in the past, the way was now open for two obviously talented men whose humanist stepfather was something of a legend in the papal service. Still, Lucerne had to act unilaterally. The pope sent the city a letter by way of his nuncio, Cardinal Volpe, requesting nominations for the post. Volpe was slow in passing it on to the Swiss authorities, and by the time he did, Segesser was already on his way to Rome with several companions, including his brother, without papal approval.

That approval was forthcoming shortly after his arrival, however, as were other honors. Jost was named a Knight of the Golden Spur by the pope. Perhaps the friends in the Vatican that the brothers had made in their earlier life in the household of their stepfather and in their own right as men who had risen in the ranks doing service in the Guard had something to do with this rapid advancement. Both had already learned how to move in high circles both among the Curia and the Roman nobility. Even when, after the unexpected nomination of Leo Kaspar von Silenen, they had withdrawn to Ravenna, they did not accept the position passively. As it became clear that the salary would not support two people, Albrecht left the position to his younger brother and returned to Switzerland. Jost also returned to Switzerland shortly thereafter, and both were highly successful in both politics and business at home.

Jost Segesser displayed the same personal finesse and administrative skills as commandant of the Swiss Guard as he had shown in private life. He quickly established order again among the guards. One sign that things were well under control is that he had the time to write regular reports on events in Rome, which both reveal the inner workings of the Curia and possess no little literary merit. One ominous development that he describes is the incursion of the Turks into the area around Pescara on Italy's eastern coast, where they destroyed several villages.[7] The pope responded by sending troops as reinforcements, among them twenty-five Swiss knights as bodyguards for the commandant, along with a few officers from the papal guards. In Rome itself, the pope and his entourage visited the main churches to pray for help against the Muslim threat.

In the same period, Pius V also sought to shore up the Church by promising a hundred thousand crowns to the king of France if he would do battle with the French Huguenots. Princes at the time were usually wary of stirring up conflicts among their people by internal religious crusades of this kind. Charles IX, the French king in 1569, was unusual in that he let himself by swayed by one faction or another, according to his momentary mood. He was in the Catholic camp when he was young and under the protection of his mother, Catherine de' Medici. It was at this point that he captured a dozen ensigns of the Huguenots and sent them to Rome, where, according to Segesser, the Swiss guards in full dress carried them to St. Peter's in celebration of the success of the Catholic armies. Shortly thereafter, however, Charles would fall under the influence of Gaspard de Coligny, a leader of the French Huguenots, before changing his mind yet again and allowing the St. Bartholomew's Day Massacre in 1570, an infamous episode in which thousands of French Protestants were killed.

In addition to his various ceremonial duties, the Swiss commandant noted a massive Turkish buildup and the preparations at Rome to deal with it. Ambassadors were sent out to Spain and Venice, among other powers, in the hope of creating an effective military alliance against the common enemy. Jost Segesser himself took an active role in this diplomacy, if somewhat by accident. He did so partly because he fell ill and had to request a leave of absence to return home for health reasons. The pope allowed this, but also asked him to carry out a mission in Switzerland: to request four to five thousand men for the battle against the Turks. The Swiss authorities were not eager to fulfill this request and suggested, instead, that if a real emergency arose later they would be quick to help. The Diets of Lucerne and Baden rejected it outright. The general feeling seems to have been that the Turkish threat to Switzerland was just too remote. Swiss leaders also feared another loss of life such as had occurred at Paliano. For the moment, it seemed more prudent to keep Swiss troops at home for the defense of their own country.

The Swiss and the Battle of Lepanto

Despite the attitude of the Swiss authorities, the Papal Swiss Guard, somewhat surprisingly for soldiers from a landlocked nation, were to participate in the naval battle against the Turks at Lepanto in the waters off Corinth on the Greek mainland on October 7, 1571. That conflict is little appreciated or even remembered today, but at the time it was an important victory, if not the dramatic turning point in European affairs that it was sometimes thought to have been. At Lepanto, the Christian forces drove back the immediate threat by the Ottoman Turks, but because of political complexities involving Venice's interests in the eastern Mediterranean, relations soon stabilized again. Yet Lepanto was in several ways the beginning of the end of the longstanding threats to Christian Europe from militant Islam. The news of the victory gave rise to celebrations all over Europe. Pope Pius V acknowledged the importance of the date by naming it the Feast of Our Lady of Victory.

Today, it may make us a bit uncomfortable to see the struggle between Europe and the Ottoman Empire cast in religious terms. It is important to realize, however, that since its founding in the seventh century, Islam had been the aggressive culture, conquering all of the Middle East, North Africa, and Spain within seventy years, and probing for soft spots among the Christian nations continuously thereafter. In the year before Lepanto, for example, the Turks had taken Cyprus from Venice. They would press on the mainland into the Balkans until the famous defeat, partly owing to Polish janissaries, outside the gates of Vienna in 1683. Memories of the outrages committed against Christians and Muslims alike during the Christian crusades of centuries earlier have tended in the West to obscure the fact that the crusaders, for all their crimes, were responding to a real threat. (Saracens invaded Rome and looted St. Peter's in 856, Muslims controlled Sicily from 902 to 1091, and Islamic raiders periodically struck Italian ports.) It was the Muslim forces of the time that were far more powerful than Christian Europe and bent on imperialist expansion into Christian lands.

The Swiss guards wound up at the Battle of Lepanto because of the conjunction of several factors. First, the pope succeeded in assembling various powers — among them the Holy See, the Knights of Malta, Spain, Venice, the Grand Duchy of Tuscany, the republic of Genoa, the duke of Savoy, Mantua, Parma, Lucca, and Ferrara — into a Holy League to fight the Turks.[8] This alone was an achievement that several previous pontiffs had pursued without success. Pius V also wanted the Swiss in the coalition, but — as noted above — Commandant Segesser could not convince them to join the other European powers.

Yet the pope found another way to inject the Swiss into the preparations for battle. Don John of Austria was the commander-in-chief of the Christian forces. Many other distinguished figures would also take part, including Miguel de Cervantes, later author of *Don Quixote,* who was wounded. Marcantonio Colonna, scion of the famous noble Roman family and an experienced warrior, was named general for the papal forces. The pope also ordered that twenty-five men from his own Swiss guards accompany Colonna as personal bodyguards.[9] They all joined with the vast flotilla of the Holy League, which numbered 208 ships and thirty thousand men, who then faced a roughly equal number of Turkish vessels and troops. But the results of the battle were very unequal in favor of the Christian forces. As was the military custom of the time, the two fleets engaged after a chivalrous, formalized procedure. When the lines of ships faced one another, one side would offer to do battle by firing a single cannon shot. If the other side chose to accept the challenge, it replied with a two-cannon volley. At Lepanto, the Turks made the first move and were immediately answered. After that, the Christian forces sang psalms together as they moved forward, and the battle quickly descended into the usual chaos and carnage.

Historians disagree about the exact numbers of losses on either side, but the basic proportions are beyond doubt. By one good estimate, the Christians lost seventeen ships and seventy-five hundred men. Fifteen Turkish ships were sunk outright and an additional 177 captured. Others were burned or ran aground. As many as thirty thousand Turks may have perished, and fifteen thousand Christian slaves, who were used as rowers in the galleys, were set free. As late as the early part of the twentieth century, this heroic triumph would be celebrated in literature, perhaps most memorably in the British writer G. K. Chesterton's poem "Lepanto":

> Above the ships are palaces of brown, black-bearded chiefs,
> And below the ships are prisons, where with multitudinous griefs,
> Christian captives sick and sunless, all a labouring race repines
> Like a race in sunken cities, like a nation in the mines.
> They are lost like slaves that sweat, and in the skies of morning hung
> The stair-ways of the tallest gods when tyranny was young.
> They are countless, voiceless, hopeless as those fallen or fleeing on
> Before the high Kings' horses in the granite of Babylon.
> And many a one grows witless in his quiet room in hell
> Where a yellow face looks inward through the lattice of his cell,
> And he finds his God forgotten, and he seeks no more a sign —
> (*But Don John of Austria has burst the battle-line!*)
> Don John pounding from the slaughter-painted poop,
> Purpling all the ocean like a bloody pirate's sloop,
> Scarlet running over on the silvers and the golds,
> Breaking of the hatches up and bursting of the holds,
> Thronging of the thousands up that labour under sea
> White for bliss and blind for sun and stunned for liberty.

The victory also led to triumphs back in sixteenth-century Rome and elsewhere. One of the Swiss involved in the fighting, Hanns Nölly of Kriens, captured two Turkish standards and sent them to the government in Lucerne, for which he received fifteen crowns in recognition of bravery and honorary citizenship for himself and his family. Jost Segesser wrote a detailed report for the Swiss authorities on how his men had fared in this adventure:

> They all acquitted themselves with honor and only one of my people, my scribe, died, God bless him; several, however, suffered light injuries because they were not very familiar with the weapons, although their injuries could have been much worse. Also, one of our men from Kriens — his name is Hanns Nölly — captured two banners from the Turks' main galley.... We recommend him to you.... [10]

Marcantonio Colonna was awarded a formal triumph in Rome similar to what the ancient Roman generals had enjoyed under the republic and the empire. He was met on the Appian Way by Commandant Segesser and the Swiss guards and led to the Church of San Sebastiano, before proceeding to the Capitol. There, as in ancient times, the commander and his troops were cheered as they marched by, preceded by the trophies they had taken from the enemy. The Roman knights and the Swiss escorted them through the crowds that had turned out to see this colorful and unusual spectacle. Forty high-ranking Turkish captives marched in the triumph and were placed in the custody of the Swiss guards. Several colorful frescoes pompously celebrating this victory adorn the walls and ceilings in the Palazzo Colonna even today.

A Long, Uneventful Period

After so much turmoil during the first century or so of its existence, the Swiss Guard entered — or endured, depending on the perspective — about two hundred years of quiet, so much so that a historian has claimed that "from the death of Jost Segesser [1592] to the occupation of Rome by the Directory [the revolutionary French government at the end of the eighteenth century] we cannot mention any event of importance" involving the guards.[11] There are several reasons for this relative quietude. To begin with, once the nation-states of Europe fully emerged in the sixteenth century, it was they who became the central actors, not the pope or the Papal States. Given the struggles in Italy in the sixteenth century, this was not an entirely unwelcome development. Furthermore, after the Wars of Religion had demonstrated to both Catholics and Protestants that it was both useless and wrong to fight with one another about matters of faith, all sides agreed under the 1648 Treaty of Westphalia that rulers could set the official religion of their land, often enough with some accommodations for minority faiths (*cuius regio, eius religio*). So religious matters after 1648 were largely taken off the table of politics. Perhaps most importantly for the guards, the Holy See established a nuncio, a kind of papal ambassador, among the Catholic cantons in Switzerland, which formalized relations in a manner that did away in large part with the Swiss commandant's traditional role as an intermediary between home and the Holy See.

Jost Segesser's very power and success as intermediary contributed to this new state of affairs. Over the course of twenty years, he played a greater role in Swiss-papal relations and politics more generally than any other occupant of his position.[12] He received many honors for this work. Pius V made him a Knight of the Golden Spur. Gregory XIII dubbed him *familiaris Suae Sanctitatis,* which might be translated as something like "of the household of His Holiness." In 1587, Sixtus V made Segesser head of all Swiss troops serving the Holy See. Pius and his successors used Segesser as an ambassador, not only to Switzerland but to various Italian jurisdictions, and he was active to such an extent in Switzerland that he was responsible for many new initiatives, not least the creation of the permanent nuncio, who would replace the commandant of the Swiss Guard as the primary diplomatic figure in relationships between Rome and Lucerne. Indeed, he was considered as a candidate for the post of papal nuncio since the Catholic cantons were afraid that a cleric might give offense to the Protestant cantons. In the end, the Vatican decided to go ahead with a cardinal, but not for any lack of ability or loyalty on the Swiss commandant's part. Jost Segesser died on June 8, 1592, during an embassy to Florence on behalf of the pope. The archduke of Tuscany, Ferdinand I de' Medici, honored him with a funeral at the Medici family's principal church in the city, San Lorenzo, where many of the Medici themselves were buried.

Years of Peace and the Altishofen Dynasty

More peaceful times led to a less agitated life and more durable leadership of the guards. Jost Segesser's son, Stephan-Alexander, had grown up in Rome and served in the Guard. As a result, he knew the ways of the papal Curia and the Swiss guards very well, and was the natural choice to follow his father as commandant.

He served in that position for thirty-seven years (1592–1629). Like his father, he also accumulated other responsibilities: in 1606, he became the ambassador of the seven Catholic cantons to the Holy See, and in 1623 he was named by the pope as commander over all the Swiss troops in papal service throughout Italy. Stephan-Alexander, for all his achievements, seems to have been a modest and retiring character, and his time as commandant passed without notable incident. Nikolaus Fleckenstein (1629–40) and Jost Fleckenstein (1640–52), members of a distinguished Lucerne family (Jost was mayor at the time of his appointment as commandant), each passed about a dozen years running the papal bodyguards. But the next significant development for the guards was to come with the beginning of a long dynasty of officers of the family Pfyffer von Altishofen, which stretched with some interruptions from 1652 to the late twentieth century.

The first member of this dynasty, Johann Rudolf, had to deal with some of the fallout of the Treaty of Westphalia, which generally reduced the presence of religion, and consequently of the papacy, in European politics. That shift also changed the need for the Swiss Guard to be a potential fighting force since the kinds of troubles that had given them an important role in the Italian wars were now largely over. As welcome as that development might be, however, it meant that the Swiss now served a mostly ceremonial function for a long period. The Vatican decided, as a result, to reduce the number of men in the Guard to 120. As far as can be judged from the records, this seems also to have had the effect of lowering morale and discipline. Protests arose over the cost of living and low pay. In one notorious incident toward the end of the 1600s, the guards and the Roman police got into a fight in a tavern (Swiss guards were exempt from the Roman tax on wine) — "sticks against halberds," as it was later described. Over the rest of the century and beyond, the guards would also tend to become less explicitly Swiss. Many of the men lived for decades in Rome, married Roman women, and had children who grew up in Italy virtually as Italians. When these children turned to the papal service to become "Swiss" guards, it was difficult to say in what sense that was true or not.

The situation by the first decades of the eighteenth century called for serious reform, and that was just what the Pfyffer von Altishofens of the time instituted. Johann Konrad (1712–27), who took over as commandant after that position had remained vacant for seven years, began the process by virtually starting over again. He had the traditional regulations of the Guard read to the men and took steps to see that the rules were followed in the performance of everyday duties. His successor, Franz Ludwig (1727–54), took on an even more deep-rooted problem, the irregularities and burdens on the guards stemming from their family lives. By this point, the barracks inside the Sant'Anna Gate, which even in modern times offer quite limited space, were overburdened by guards with several dependents and by survivors of guards who had died. Franz Ludwig eliminated the practice of allowing survivors to live in official quarters. More seriously, he established the rule, which still remains in effect, that halberdiers must be unmarried to be admitted to the corps and must remain unmarried until they have reached officer's rank. Even then, the number of people allowed to marry would be strictly controlled. These could not have been popular measures, but they helped reestablish a certain minimum military discipline in a force that had limited resources. Discipline would soon prove to be much needed.

In the short term, however, the guards had relatively minor problems to contend with. For example, Clement XIV (pope 1669–1774), a kind-hearted man, found himself one day being harangued by a Scottish Presbyterian in St. Peter's. This ardent, or mad, soul went through the usual litany of charges against the papacy — the seven-headed beast, mother of harlots, etc. The Swiss guards took the man into custody and discovered that he had come all the way from his native land in order to convert the poor deluded pope. He was released and put on a ship for home by the Swiss guards when Clement, generously praising what he was sure were the man's good intentions, paid for his passage.[13]

The Popes, the Swiss Guard, and the French Revolution

Toward the end of the eighteenth century, the papal throne was occupied by a series of holy and decent men who unfortunately proved unable to stand up to the virulent revolutionary forces stirring in Europe, especially in France. This situation would have a significant impact on the Swiss Guard. Benedict XIV (pope 1740–58), for example, was distinguished for his humility, good temper, willingness to listen to new ideas, and gifts as an administrator. He often visited parishes in Rome, "sometimes incognito, wearing a wig and tricorne hat."[14] But revolutionary opponents of the Church took advantage of his mildness both in Rome and elsewhere. His two immediate successors, Clement XIII and Clement XIV, continued along the same line and found themselves forced to preside over the suppression of the Jesuit order, first in France, then in its entirety. These concessions to the more virulent facets of European opinion did not win the papacy any friends, as they were intended to do. To the contrary, the display of weakness and pliability encouraged still greater pressures on the Church.

A somewhat stronger figure, Giannangelo Braschi became Pope Pius VI in 1775. Braschi showed many of the traditional airs and attitudes of the old Roman nobility, which served him in good stead as he began to develop the infrastructure of the city. But Pius VI was no match for the forces unleashed by the French Revolution in 1789. To begin with, his diplomatic skills were limited. After much hesitation, he condemned the new French constitution, which led to clashes in Paris between factions that opposed the Church and those that supported it.

As would happen in later revolutions, anti-religious forces were stirred up by the new regime with the usual caricatures of immorality in religious houses and of greed among the hierarchy. Demonstrations occurred outside churches, convents were entered, and nuns insulted. The pope, having blundered by too blunt a response to the new political situation in France, now went to the opposite extreme and remained silent during the turmoil, believing that if he were to speak out against the rioters, it would only make the situation worse for French Catholics.

Pius VI's misjudgments were matched, however, by the misguided arrogance of the representatives of the new French regime in Rome, who, like their counterparts elsewhere, had explicitly been sent to spread revolutionary fervor. Their presence in Rome had the opposite effect. Though the Church had its enemies even at home, the Roman people almost universally came to an early and deep dislike of the revolutionaries. Stories of revolutionary outrages in Paris offended the Romans, and they took still greater offense at the way the French envoys strutted around the city prominently displaying revolutionary symbols. It did not help the French case that the disorders in France had led to a drop-off in tourism to Rome with all the economic consequences that brought with it for Roman shopkeepers and their suppliers in the Italian countryside. In January of 1793, after growing tensions, two French representatives drove down the Corso, the main street for socializing in Rome at the time, with a revolutionary flag flying from the carriage. The Roman people had finally had enough and stoned them. One was stabbed in the stomach and died. Mobs moved against French outposts throughout the city, and large demonstrations took place in favor of the pope and the Church.[15]

At the moment, there was little the French could do in response, but three years later the Directory appointed a military commander for Italy who would avenge that death and more, Napoleon Bonaparte. As was his custom, Napoleon portrayed his entry into Italy as an idealistic attempt to liberate "the descendants of Brutus and the Scipios," and "to free the Roman people from their long slavery."[16] As was also his custom, he did not entirely carry out the orders he had received, but turned them to his own ultimate advantage as he began his climb from being a servant of the Revolution to becoming its absolute master. The Directory had ordered him to transfer as much wealth as possible from Italy to France, since the French state was nearly bankrupt under the administration of the revolutionaries. It also wanted Napoleon to enter Rome and depose the pope. Napoleon was only too happy to oblige his superiors on the first count after he had taken possession of important parts of the Papal States such as Bologna, Ferrara, and the Romagna. His forces packed up priceless works of ancient and modern art for shipment to France along with masses of gold and silver and numerous diamonds, emeralds, rubies, sapphires, and pearls. But Napoleon calculated that deposing the pope might lead other powers, especially Naples, to move into central Italy. So instead of invading, he made his brother Joseph French ambassador in the city.

This arrangement, intended to encourage papal French sympathizers, soon erupted into violence. The French, some of their friends from northern Italy, and the Romans who wanted a republic organized a demonstration over high food prices in the city. Papal troops responded to the disorder and, in the course of containing the demonstrators, killed two of them. The next day, December 28, 1797, some of the demonstrators went to see Joseph Bonaparte at the French embassy. Papal cavalry attacked them there and, later, outside the embassy, shot and killed Léon Duphot, a French adjutant-general sent to Rome to foment revolution, who had emerged from the building with a sword. In Paris, the Directory took this as an opportunity to carry out the long desired invasion of Rome. It was easily accomplished in February 13, 1798. The new French commander, General Louis-Alexandre Berthier, took possession of Castel Sant'Angelo, arrested the papal commanders, and disarmed the papal forces. On February 15, the pope was informed that he was no longer the ruler of the city, and the Roman Republic was announced. On

February 16, the French replaced the Swiss as the pope's personal bodyguard and raised the French flag over the Holy See. With even greater aggressiveness (and resentment by the Romans as a result), they turned the angel on top of Castel Sant'Angelo into "the Liberating Genius of France" by painting it French colors and giving it a cap of liberty.[17] The pope was "informed" that he was to leave the city. The eighty-two-year-old pontiff departed for France. Among the nineteen persons who were allowed by the French to accompany him into exile was Ludwig Pfyffer von Altishofen, the Swiss commandant.[18]

Pfyffer reported on all these events to the government in Lucerne, which allowed him to dismiss the men under his command. Most of them returned home. But Switzerland itself was not immune to the designs of France. Before Lucerne was even able to reply to Pfyffer's report, their own capital, Bern, was occupied by revolutionary troops, who proclaimed the Helvetic Republic and dissolved the old confederation. The Catholic cantons resisted and organized armed forces but were overcome by the superior numbers of the revolutionaries. So the Switzerland to which the guards returned was in essentially the same hostile hands as the Rome that they had just left. The new republic lasted five years (1798–1803) and operated, as did the Roman Republic, under a constitution modeled on the French constitution. During that period, Pope Pius VI died (August 29, 1799), a prisoner of the Directory at Valence.

The French forces, however, had overextended themselves. Most of the troops in Italy had to be reassigned to Switzerland and Germany to prevent loss of French control in those countries. The Roman Republic came to an end before it was even two years old. Austria and Naples moved rapidly to recover former papal territories. The same month, November 1799, saw the end of the republic and the opening at Venice of the conclave to elect the next pope. Pius VII (Giorgio Barnaba Chiaramonti), who moved to Rome on July 3, 1800, would guide the Church through the rest of the Napoleonic period and beyond. Chiaramonti had always shown some sympathies with movements for liberty and equality; he had no qualms, however, about trying to defend the freedoms of the Church. Napoleon won an important battle over the Austrians at Marengo just before the pope's return to the Holy City, which gained him control over parts of the Papal States again. Under the circumstances, France and the Holy See agreed to a concordat that specified relations between them. Napoleon, now the first consul, agreed to allow Catholics to worship without hindrance in France. The French retained a portion of the Italian territory that they had occupied, but returned a portion to the pope as well.

Another Restoration

Pius VII, perhaps as a way of trying to bolster his independence, asked a member of the Am Rhyn family of Lucerne to restore the Swiss Guard, a request quickly carried out. The process was relatively easy because there were still thirty-six guards and five officers who had remained in Rome during the Revolution. In a further sign of a return to normalcy, Karl Pfyffer von Altishofen became commandant of the reconstituted force and within a short time had doubled the number of men and officers.[19] But such small forces could not really expect to resist Napoleon if he became serious about taking control of Rome again. He decided to do that shortly after he crowned himself emperor in 1804, with the pope in attendance. It was clear that he intended to annex Italy to the French Empire, declare Rome a "free imperial city," and subordinate the pope and the Church to his rule. He did all that, and with such a heavy hand, that the Romans would come to hate the French. When imperial French forces arrived at the Quirinale Palace, the pope's summer residence, in 1809 under the command of Colonel Etienne Radet, the pope did not want the Swiss to shed their blood in vain, and he ordered them to lay down their arms. Once again, a pope was carted off into exile and the Swiss Guard disbanded.

As in the first exile, however, the pope's return followed quickly on events elsewhere. Napoleon's rule and the empire he had created came to an end on April 4, 1814, when he abdicated. Several weeks later the pope was welcomed back into Rome by the populace, and Karl Pfyffer von Altishofen reconstituted the troops over which he had held command only a few years before. The pope generously granted asylum in Rome to Napoleon's mother, Letizia, two of his brothers (Lucien and Joseph), his sister Elsa, and several Napoleonic officials after the dissolution of the empire. This put a charitable end to the tumultuous Napoleonic period in Europe, the Church, and the Swiss Guard. But the social revolution that was to occur in all of Europe to a greater or lesser extent during the nineteenth century would lead to a permanent and far more radical change in the status of the pope as a temporal ruler. The Italians were among the last people in Europe to unify themselves under a nation-state roughly coterminous with the areas where Italian — or at least one of its numerous dialects — was spoken. And when they did, it would take away the last vestiges of the pope's direct political power, but he would emerge from that seeming loss purified as a moral and spiritual force in the world.

Chapter Six

The Guard during the Unification of Italy and the Pope's Imprisonment in the Vatican

ON NOVEMBER 15, 1848, Count Pellegrino Rossi, a haughty man who had just two months earlier become the leader of the newly created constitutional government of the Papal States, arrived at the Palazzo della Cancelleria, the palace in which a session of the Roman Council of Deputies was about to begin. As he walked through the courtyard without protection between two lines of an honor guard consisting of men who had recently returned from the wars in the northern province of Lombardy to free Italy from foreign domination, one man struck out at him with a dagger. Another stabbed him in the throat. Rossi, a well-known liberal whose books had been prohibited by the Vatican and who had a Protestant wife,[1] had nonetheless been accepted as a political leader in the Papal States by Pope Pius IX because he seemed to hold out some hope for maintaining order in the revolutionary atmosphere that was breaking out all over Europe in 1848. His Julius Caesar-like assassination, however, set in motion a change in the Papal States as great as the change Caesar's death had brought to the old Roman Republic. The changes would deeply touch the long-term fortunes of the papacy, for good and for bad, and of the Swiss Guard in its services to the popes.

In the short term, Rossi's death put the pope and the guards in immediate danger of their lives. By the next morning, it was clear that few reliable allies remained with them in the city. Only two cardinals had come to the Quirinale Palace — today the headquarters of the Italian president, then one of the pope's summer residences within Rome when the Vatican was too uncomfortable. In the square outside the palace, elements from the Roman police force, the carabinieri (state police), the city of Rome's Civic Guard, and even some papal troops had joined with the revolutionaries. The Roman people, as usual, waited to see who might emerge victorious. Inside the palace, there were only eight or nine foreign ambassadors, a few priests, some papal servants, the pope, and seventy Swiss guards (in contingents of about a dozen at each guard post). Fifty more Swiss guards were stationed at the Vatican. When the quickly named interim leader of the Council of Deputies, Giuseppe Galletti, tried to explain to the crowd — from the Quirinale balcony from which the pope usually imparted his blessing — why Pius IX could not give in to force, the crowd became even more enraged and dispersed in search of weapons. Six thousand of them returned, heavily armed, an hour later.[2] Bullets began flying. The pope remained calm inside the Quirinale, though he was far from safe. Sharpshooters who set themselves up outside the palace sent bullets inside the building with deadly accuracy. Bishop Palma, the pope's secretary for "Latin letters," was killed when he showed himself at one of the windows. The Roman Civic Guard brought a field gun within range of the palace, but for the moment refrained from using it.

The Swiss went through some hair-raising experiences. Franz Xaver Leopold Meyer von Schauensee, who had been named acting commandant just a few months earlier, was in charge of security at the Quirinale and was directly involved, along with several other Swiss officers, in the tumult that ensued.[3] A small number of the Swiss were able to repel the crowd's first attempt to enter the Quirinale after hearing of the pope's refusal to grant their demands. Sword blows were exchanged, but the guards at the main portals held. Stones were also flying everywhere by that point, however, and some members of the crowd tried to use the resulting confusion as a diversion to allow them to climb through windows. At this point, Galletti and Pietro Sterbini, a colleague in the Chamber of Deputies, appeared again on the balcony to say that, though the pope would not agree to demands, he was willing to allow the demands to be discussed in the legislative chamber. Despite this concession, the crowd became further incensed and tried to storm the palace once more. The Swiss had been forbidden by their officers to fire on the crowd. They did, however, as one of them wrote later, "fire some ten or twelve shots over their heads and chased away the crowd in the blink of an eye. In two minutes, there were no longer any men in the Piazza."[4]

In the temporary lull that followed, it became clear that the situation was worse than had first appeared and was far from resolved. Another bishop had a head wound from a bullet that grazed his skull. Some of the Swiss guards had minor bruises, and two of the City Guards lay wounded on the street outside the palace. Under the circumstances, it was remarkable that there had not been many more casualties. The Swiss commandant rightly claimed in a letter sometime later that, except for the places where it had been unavoidable, they had not used any more firepower against the people than was absolutely necessary. His restraint and that of his men, however, was lost on the Italian mobs. Some of them had cried out when shots had begun to fly — only in response to threats to the Holy Father and the Quirinale Palace — "The Swiss are killing the people! To arms!" It was unfair and would lead to further bloodshed, but such are the confusions and passions of large groups in situations of violent conflict.

In fact, several of the Swiss guards had some sympathy for the attempt to set up a democratic republic in Italy and had expressed as much openly. In this, they were not at all at odds with their own superiors. Pius IX himself, to great acclaim around the world, had begun his papacy by showing many signs of wanting to explore that possibility. He reversed many of the policies of his reactionary predecessor, Gregory XVI (Gregory was so opposed to modern innovations that he had forbidden gas lamps within the city of Rome and trains within the Papal States, calling the latter *chemins d'Enfer,* "paths of Hell," a play on the French for trains, *chemins de fer*). Pius IX immediately encouraged the development of both. Ironically, just two years before this assault, the pope had appeared in the balcony overlooking the very same piazza next to the Quirinale Palace and had been enthusiastically cheered by a large Roman crowd for having freed about four hundred prisoners held for political reasons by Pope Gregory, among them both Galletti and Sterbini. In the two intervening years, however, events driven by popular passions had soured the pope on popular government and soured the people on the pope. It was a pattern similar to the struggle between liberals and conservatives going on all over Europe during the nineteenth century.

When the rioting resumed, the insurrectionists were able to capture the Swiss Commandant Meyer. They put a logical question to him: "Who are you for, the People or the Pope?" Without missing a beat, Meyer gave the reply: "I am for duty [*Pflicht*]."[5] A noble answer, but one that angered the rebels. They put him in front of the field gun and prepared to fire. He took a look at it and maintained his composure: "I know this cannon, it's the *San Pietro.* When it fires, history will recount how on November 16 the Romans killed a brave officer who with twenty-five comrades at Vicenza wrested this very gun out of the hands of the Austrians." Since the Romans, who were seeking independence, wanted to be free from the foreign domination of then-powerful Austria as much as they wanted freedom from the pope's political rule over central Italy, they now found themselves in a dilemma over what to do with Meyer. They could not execute someone who had fought so bravely against the Austrians, so they decided to keep him in custody until matters could be sorted out. The other Swiss officers later reported that it was thanks to Galletti's intervention that the commandant was set free. Meyer himself never spoke much about what happened to him in captivity, except for a few general remarks.

The situation seems to have evolved like this: the crowd started to grow very angry, firing off shots and hurling stones, and shouted "Down with Pius IX! Death to the Swiss! Long Live the Republic!" The leaders of the republicans themselves were only able to keep the crowds under control by firing cannon shots over their heads. The pope, who had remained intransigent during all this, finally agreed to concessions to head off even worse violence. He approved a list of ministers for the new government but announced that he wanted nothing to do with that regime. Galletti again spoke to the crowd from the Quirinale balcony to announce the pope's concessions. This finally appeased the insurgents. He also urged them to forget their anger toward the Swiss, since the guards and their countrymen had fought for Italy at Vicenza. The rebels freed Meyer, and the resentment against the Swiss seemed to have dissipated. But the next morning, a new delegation came to the pope with word that the people were still furious and were about to mount a demonstration unless Pius relieved the Swiss of their duty. It was harsh treatment for troops who had walked a careful line defending the pope and not shedding any more blood than necessary (while sustaining no fatalities themselves and only one man wounded). The pope had no other choice, however. He ordered Meyer to return to quarters with his men. The Roman newspapers reported on their departure and replacement by the Civic Guard, who now effectively held the pope under house arrest.

The Pope's Escape to Gaeta

Pius IX somehow soon managed to escape by putting on dark glasses and slipping into the carriage of the Bavarian ambassador, who was visiting him. The ambassador helped him make his way to Gaeta, a small fortress city along the coast south of Rome just inside the Kingdom of the Two Sicilies, an area administered by Naples.[6] For the guards, the situation was probably reminiscent of the early days of their existence when Clement VII had fled the Spanish imperial troops and the more recent abductions of the two popes by French revolutionary forces and Napoleon in 1799 and 1809. The Roman people, too, seem to have regarded the episode as another temporary setback for the papacy rather than a permanent change. But it proved to be a little bit of both and, in the long run, the prelude to the complete end to the pope's temporal rule. In the short run, various powers — Austria, France, Spain, and Naples itself — operating within Italy had interests in making sure the pope returned to Rome; they began to organize their forces to that end.

The Swiss Guard played a more active role than usual in these developments. As early as January of 1849 — just a month after the pontiff's escape — Acting Commandant Meyer was called to Gaeta to talk with the pope. Pius IX gave him orders to travel to northern Italy and to assemble the two regiments of foreign volunteers who had come to Italy from all over the Catholic world to defend the pope and the Papal States from various threats. The Swiss commander was then to lead the troops south through the Papal States to the border with Naples. They would then be used along with the troops of foreign powers to force the pope's return to Rome — clearly, no easy matter under the circumstances. Meyer took a ship to the northern port of Livorno and then traveled overland to Bologna. There he presented the pope's request to General Latour, who commanded one of the regiments, but Latour already had trouble on his hands. And when word of the papal plans got around the city, there emerged a real threat of a popular uprising. The cardinal legate and other prominent leaders in Bologna convinced Latour not to withdraw the troops, which would only further encourage rebellion. Assembling the other regiment proved hopeless as well. In fact, Meyer barely escaped capture by Italian revolutionaries.

While he was in northern Italy, he took advantage of the opportunity to make a brief visit and meditate on his fallen Swiss comrades in the graveyard at Vicenza. Then he moved swiftly across the northern part of the peninsula, going all the way to Trieste, where he met with a general from Naples who had himself just been on a recruiting mission to Vienna in search of troops to carry out the papal restoration. He too had had little luck. Both men returned to Gaeta with the bad news. Relief was to come from a different quarter. Meyer went to the port city of Civitavecchia on the coast north of Rome to await further developments. He was there when French general Charles Oudinot landed and marched on Rome. After a bloody battle on the Janiculum, a hill with a panoramic view of the city, Oudinot and the French overcame the Italian revolutionary leader Giuseppe Garibaldi and his Redshirts and entered Rome on July 3, 1849, through the Porta San Pancrazio. The leaders of the Italian Republic fled, many to England. Garibaldi retreated with forty-five hundred of his men. Meyer arrived in the city two days later and had to take lodging in a hotel since his quarters in the Vatican were being used as a kind of field hospital. That night he watched the celebration of the return of papal rule from the heights of Castel Sant'Angelo: the papal flag was raised over the castle, the whole city was lit up, and hundred-cannon volleys went off.

Meyer and the Guard Prior to 1849

Meyer immediately set to work reconstituting the Guard. He did so with the energy and ability that he had shown throughout his whole career in Switzerland and Italy as a military leader. It was providential that he had been acting commandant the year before because, since the 1815 Congress of Vienna, the Swiss Guard had been in a state of constant turmoil, largely because of lapses or outright misbehavior of officers and men alike, beginning with the commanders. Money had always been tight for the ordinary halberdiers in the Guard. Charges began to be raised in 1815, however, and continued over the next three decades that there was mismanagement and perhaps even dishonesty on the part of Karl Leodegar Pfyffer von Altishofen (commandant 1800–1834) and his son Martin (commandant 1834–47). In 1819, for example, more than twenty guards signed a complaint that was sent to Vatican officials that spelled out a long list of grievances and alleged irregularities, some perhaps real, others imagined. At a distance of almost two centuries, it is difficult to know exactly how much of the discontent to assign to possibly shady dealings and how much arose from personalities, rivalries, and resentments among the various actors. By the time Pius IX brought in Acting Commandant Meyer, however, there was a long and undeniable record of widespread disorders that reflected poorly on the guards.

A former chaplain to the guards, a Father Erasmus Baumgartner, informed the Diet of Lucerne in writing that "the Swiss Guard, once so honorable, will bring shame on the Swiss name if they are not restored to order."[7] He went on to detail the haphazard way in which officers were being assigned and the resulting insubordination, quarrels, lax discipline, and even irreligiousness among the troops. The only remedy that offered itself for such deep, standing abuses was for the commanders somehow to engineer a return to the older order. In response to these charges, Lucerne ordered Karl Pfyffer to make a comprehensive report, in particular about stories that non-Swiss officers were serving along with Swiss. Pfyffer made some lame excuses about poor recruiting and financial difficulties, but had nothing to say about the various disciplinary issues that urgently needed to be addressed.

The guards did not even have a proper agreement (*Kapitulation*) with the Holy See at this point. After the fall of Napoleon, the 1815 Congress of Vienna established the basic shape of the new international order for Europe, but for the rest of the century the revolutionary sentiments first unleashed in France alternated with conservative reactions. Switzerland asserted its historic neutrality in European affairs. Individual cantons could work out military agreements with foreign powers, but these had to be presented to the Swiss Diet for approval. No such agreement had been signed between the Swiss and Pius VII because he was occupied with trying to restore order in the Papal States following his return from capture by the French. For the pope, it was enough for the Swiss to continue at their traditional duties for the time being. This return to business as usual might have been temporarily workable had there been no disputes, and the pope may even have had in mind that it would be premature to do anything of a substantive nature about the Swiss until he had a better idea of the needs of the papacy in post-Napoleonic Europe.

It was only with the election of Leo XII in 1823 that the situation changed. As was the usual custom, Lucerne wrote to congratulate the new pope on the occasion of his assumption of the chair of Peter, but included in the same document a request that the Swiss relationship with the Holy See be put into more regular order. By this point, the Vatican was ready to do so; the following year Leo sent Karl Pfyffer to Switzerland on a dual mission. First, he was to open discussions about the *Kapitulation*. More urgent in the pope's mind, however, was the need for two thousand Swiss troops who would reinforce his position by their presence but would also furnish a model for all the papal forces in Italy to develop the kind of strict military discipline and devotion to duty for which the Swiss were famous. Lucerne immediately gave him indications that such an arrangement could be possible, even though other European powers were seeking similar help. The Swiss made use of the occasion, however, to link the raising of the two thousand troops with the renewal of the *Kapitulation*, since there was general unrest about the existing relationship with the Holy See. Pope Leo commended the historic loyalty of the guards, and in the new *Kapitulation* specified that their numbers should be raised from a little over a hundred to two hundred, and kept at that level. Payments comparable to past arrangements were spelled out, and Lucerne received special powers, as in the past, to recruit and monitor who was admitted to service.

The Vatican officially approved of the new *Kapitulation* on October 18, 1824. In January of 1825, Lucerne agreed to its terms as well, and when word was received in Rome of the Swiss agreement, the whole corps of guards swore allegiance to the pope in a special ceremony in the *sala regia* of the Vatican palace.[8] But the goals laid out in the agreement were easier to formulate than to realize. Over the next few years, the Swiss force in the Vatican generally totaled around 125; and in the whole period, the highest number reached was 197, three short of the size the pope had wished. The primary competition came from Naples, which was vigorously recruiting Swiss soldiers and offering incentives for them to enlist as mercenaries further south than Rome. The papal guards seem to have tried to make service more attractive by including opportunities for study in Rome during the period of service. Also, recruits who found the service uncongenial after they arrived in Rome were allowed to resign without great difficulty, which was not a problem when recruits were plentiful. When they were not, it could lead to embarrassments.

By and large, however, the new agreement spelled out reasonable terms for service, including a provision for pensions. Its main failing, however, was that the commandant was put in charge of administration of all funds as well as recruiting. The Vatican had budgeted for two hundred men, and the funds designated for these positions started to find their way into "bonuses" for certain officers and other unusual categories, even though the force never numbered two hundred. The average halberdier particularly felt the brunt of these irregularities. Some seem to have tried to eke out a little more personal income by not replacing worn uniforms and keeping the difference in the amount assigned for that purpose. Their appearance and deportment suffered (some were seen going out to guard duty with their uniforms over their arms) so that the commandant had to order the ranking officer at each post to check that uniforms were in proper order and smartly worn. One reason for the problem was that many guards were married, and this placed added financial burdens on them. In the past, the number of married guards had usually been carefully restricted for precisely this reason, but some laxness in the administration seems to have allowed the number of married men to increase beyond what was prudent.

The commandant, however, did try to improve living conditions by new construction in the guards' quarters and by orders for healthier food and watch stations better protected from the weather. From the outside, the situation seemed to present certain problems but to be still within normal bounds. That appearance proved to be an illusion. Most of the commandant's efforts were on paper only. He seems by all accounts to have had a near obsession with hunting, and he absented himself from the day-to-day operations of the guards for long periods, leaving his sons in control while he pursued his favorite pastime. By the late 1820s when all this was occurring, Commandant Karl Pfyffer was in his sixties and had served as commandant for almost thirty years. Sheer age and weariness clearly had something to do with his failures in command. But that does not entirely excuse him from the minimal responsibility of seeing to it that the people to whom he delegated authority were fulfilling their roles. As it turned out, his sons were very different personalities and had very different effects within the guards. The oldest, Ignaz, was somewhat impulsive and high-handed, and it did not help matters that he and Ludwig, the third son, often operated on their own authority, causing resentment in the ranks. Martin, the middle of the three, showed himself to be much more level-headed and likable, but of sometimes unreliable judgment.

This arrangement led to an unfortunate outbreak in October of 1827. Several mid-level officers rebelled against the disorderly circumstances — in particular, a newly minted rule about how the bonuses granted on the anniversary of the pope's coronation were to be distributed — and tried to speak with the commandant. He was, as usual, hunting. His son Ignaz, who was serving as quartermaster, rudely rejected the officers' claims. When they returned again, he said he could not see them because he was ill. The commander learned of all this by the next day and wanted those guilty of insubordination arrested. He wisely asked his son Martin, who had an easier manner, to carry this out. But Martin foolishly passed the job on to Ignaz, who turned the event into yet another cause for grievance. In the guards' barracks, he lost control of himself and began shouting at other guards who now joined the initial group of officers in protest. He actually struck one of them, which led to even more general insubordination. The commandant was at Albano during all this, not far outside Rome. When he learned of what had transpired, he did not return to the city to settle matters, a misstep that caused the situation to spin further out of control.

    The following day, a staff sergeant accompanied by several veteran soldiers tried to arrest one of the rebels in his quarters. The discontented guards had clearly anticipated this move. As the sergeant entered, a whistle blew and guards rushed out from every direction to prevent the arrest. The sergeant retreated in the face of overwhelming numbers. Several of the rebels now took their complaint to the Vatican *maggiordomo,* a certain Monsignor Marazzani, who was understanding but firm that military discipline had to be observed. He promised to send a report to the pope. This invitation led to a drawing up of grievances — some exaggerated, others mistaken, but many well-taken — by a priest representing the aggrieved guards. The document went so far as to claim that Ignaz and Ludwig were tyrannical and, even worse, secret Protestants — Zwinglians and Lutherans. Their father, the commandant, was accused of withholding funds intended for equipment for his own personal use. The letter of complaint closed with a request that the pope nullify the current agreement between Switzerland and the Vatican, which had done the guardsmen no good, and that he appoint a new leader, since they would no longer obey their "bandit-commander."

    Such high-handedness on the part of the Swiss won them no sympathy from the pope or his Curia, and some of the more prudent guards soon regretted that the document had ever been composed and apologized for it. Commandant Pfyffer again asked his son Martin to set things in order. Martin dismissed three of the ringleaders and tried to rectify some of the problems that had led to the uprising. His father, however, did not show himself in the barracks. There may have been good reason, of a sort, for this: according to some reports, if he had, it would not have gone well for him. Although he was absolved of any wrongdoing by the pope, Leo XII finally intervened and expressed his desire to see the Swiss guards return to their usual orderliness and discipline. He instructed the guards' *maggiordomo* that no new regulations were to be introduced without prior approval by the Vatican, a clear limitation on the commandant's powers. There was more. The commandant was ordered to dismiss his hotheaded son Ignaz as quartermaster and to get approval for future appointments. The pope also ordered monetary fines and restriction to quarters, as well as expulsions and harsher penalties, for those who had led the insurrection.

The Lucerne Diet demanded an explanation of all this from Pfyffer. In another sign of his weak grasp of the situation, instead of sending a full report he sent Ignaz, who had been brought up in Rome and could not speak German. He presented an almost comic account of events, in Italian, that tried to blame everything on lower officers and even on the moral attitudes unleashed by the French Revolution, which he does not seem to have realized made the commandant and himself look simply ridiculous. The commandant later sent along similar rationalizations that only made things appear even worse. In mid-1828, almost thirty Swiss guards resigned and took up contract military service in Genoa — another blow to Pfyffer's reputation. The pope requested that he set the number of guards at one hundred, only half of what had been provided for in the 1825 *Kapitulation* between Switzerland and the Holy See, which further upset the Diet in Lucerne. In the midst of this turmoil, Leo XII died and Lucerne asked his successor, Pius VIII, to return as soon as possible to the original agreement specifying two hundred members of the guards.

Commandant Martin Pfyffer

All this uproar and tension seems to have undermined Pfyffer's health. He fell ill after a day hunting and died. In spite of his many failings, he had not entirely damaged his family's reputation. In fact, after his death, more than a hundred officers and enlisted men asked the Lucerne Diet to nominate Martin Pfyffer, Karl's middle son, as commandant. Martin had occupied several posts in the guards over many years and, as has already been seen, was a very different man from his elder brother, Ignaz. His character was distinguished enough that it quickly overcame any lingering resentments among the guards and any doubts in the Holy See. Pope Gregory XVI named him commandant in January of 1835. Martin struck all the right notes in his first address to his men, urging them to remember that they were soldiers and Swiss, and that they had been called to high service.

Yet the reality that followed fell far short of this vision. The commandant himself appears, like his father, to have been lax. Unauthorized persons were allowed by the guards to enter the Vatican grounds — a very serious lapse. Guards were found renting out a room at the Quirinale Palace; others got into trouble (one was even killed) because of escapades late at night after curfew. There were financial lapses similar to those that had taken place under his father. The commandant spent money on things not allowed for in the agreement with the Holy See. Financial oversight was so weak — maybe intentionally so — that the guards' administration sometimes continued to receive monthly pay from the pope for members no longer in service. These and other failings were detailed in a report by Giovanni Rusconi, who had been appointed by the Vatican secretary of state to analyze the whole situation. Rusconi pointed out that the small Swiss contingent was receiving large sums — 60,702 *scudi* and 25 ½ *bajocchi* — yet seemed incapable of carrying out its appointed tasks in proper fashion. He further specified that one of the reasons for this was that they were no longer Swiss; many were already second-generation inhabitants of Italy, and 90 percent were Roman citizens. Several did double duty. They worked as papal guards and moonlighted as security personnel in the private homes of various Roman princes and nobles, or moved back and forth in the two services. Too many guards were married, which meant that they had children and other dependents, and the financial burdens these brought with them. All of these things helped explain the perpetual penury and squalid living conditions among the guards.

They also reflected badly on the commandant and his officers, of course. Complaints signed by dozens of the halberdiers were on file with the Holy See, mostly having to do with the mishandling of funds designated for vacations, pensions, burials, and the widows of deceased guards. The commandant had failed to file yearly reports, as was required by regulations, about these financial matters. News of all this had made its way back to Lucerne, which demanded an explanation. Martin tried, but was unable to give anything but a very weak one, citing a lack of home addresses for halberdiers or regulations requiring him to hold off payments for various reasons. The Vatican, too, was dissatisfied with what were clearly evasions. Rusconi and others suggested that there was only one solution: disbanding the guards because the situation could not be remedied. There may have been some Italian military prejudice against the Swiss in this final recommendation. Yet it took an outside investigator like Rusconi by this point to get to the bottom of the problem. Martin Pfyffer did the honorable thing. He asked the pope to allow him to resign for reasons of ill health, a proposition that was immediately accepted by Pius IX, who further announced that he would personally select a replacement.

Meyer's Appointment to Command

Happily, the pope would soon announce that he had chosen Franz Leopold Meyer von Schauensee, who would turn out to be the heroic leader during the tumult at the Quirinal Palace just a few months later. Though the direct choice of commandant by the pope represented a loss of participation for Swiss authorities, who up to this point had usually offered the pope a list of three candidates, at least it made clear that the pope had not given serious thought to the possibility of disbanding the Swiss Guard. Instead, he chose to address problems by two simultaneous approaches: some new blood as commandant, who now would be chosen from Lucerne only "if possible," and a reform of the regulations for the guards, which in the past had simply give the commandant too much arbitrary control, especially in financial matters. A commission was set up to revise the latter. The commission would among its first recommendations specify that only true Swiss raised in Switzerland could become guards. Even recruits from the Ticino, an Italian-speaking canton, were forbidden, perhaps out of fear that they would fall into the same bad habits as the Italianized guards of the past few decades. Strict regulations about age (eighteen to twenty-five), height (five feet four inches), and marital status (generally, unmarried) of recruits were also instituted. Financial procedures, especially what to do with excess monthly funds, which now went into an account until their proper use was determined, were clearly spelled out.

All this, necessary as it was, seems to have produced some upset back in Lucerne. The government there was already seeking to curtail all foreign military service (i.e., mercenary contracts) and went so far as to order the return of all Swiss troops from duty abroad by 1849. As far as the papal guards in particular were concerned, the Lucerne regime seems to have regarded the new regulations as an abrogation of the earlier agreement with the Holy See. Eighty-six Swiss guards, however, signed a letter to the Swiss authorities explaining that the specific honor of papal service should not be lumped together with other mercenary services. In addition, they welcomed the changes to their constitution. Though the guards had their own ideas as to who among them should be selected commandant, they were hardly disappointed when the pope decided provisionally to bring in the distinguished outsider, Meyer von Schauensee. Lucerne seemed reasonably satisfied as well.

And no wonder. At the time of his selection, Meyer was serving as the commander of the Second Papal Foreign Regiment. The Papal States had always had troops for defensive purposes, even if they were not always successful against the major European powers. Napoleon, a good judge of military might, remarked that the moral prestige of the pope gave him the equivalent of "a corps of 200,000 men."[9] Yet popes could not rely solely on their moral standing, especially when the Italian peninsula was being eyed by outside powers. Furthermore, the nineteenth century was a period of great turmoil throughout Europe. The French Revolution and its reversal by Napoleon in the First Empire had given rise to conflicting social currents within France and elsewhere. Democratic sentiment spread, only to be countered by conservative forces that saw in the bloody Terror that slaughtered about forty thousand French immediately following the Revolution a murderous spirit that seemed intrinsic to continental democracy. The popes, who had seen two of their predecessors abducted by the French and many Catholics persecuted or martyred by revolutionary democracy, took a dim view of alleged social progress. There were revolutionary outbursts in 1830, 1848, and 1870. It was in the latter two of these outbursts that the Papal States were threatened and finally abolished by the move toward Italian unification.

Acting Commandant Meyer came from a line of distinguished military men, one of whom had served in the Swiss Guard during the seventeenth century, and added greater luster to their legacy in front-line battles during the tumultuous years of the midnineteenth century. He was born and grew up in Lucerne, and at fifteen he entered the city's *Auszugsbataillon* as a second lieutenant. He moved quickly up the ranks in various Swiss forces until in June 1832, at age twenty-three, he was called to serve in the Second Papal Foreign Regiment. Over the course of sixteen years, he was assigned to one position of command after another, receiving high praise from his superiors at every point. In 1843, he fought alongside his fellow countrymen in Switzerland against insurrectionists (so-called *Franc-tireurs* or *Freischärler*) and received the "Gratitude of the Fatherland" from the commanding general. When he returned to the pope's service in 1845, he was given command over the papal garrison at Rimini, then Forlì and Urbino. Northern Italy at the time was subject to uprisings and periodic incursions and had to maintain independence from marauding foreign powers, especially the Austrian emperor. Meyer distinguished himself during one rebellion in Rimini and received a gold medal for bravery. He wanted to return to Switzerland after that battle to fight for the Catholic cause in Switzerland's own internal conflicts, but was deterred by several considerations, not least that his return would make it appear that papal troops were involved in a civil conflict within Switzerland, not a good strategy for a country already sharply divided between Protestants and Catholics.

In 1848, revolution broke out all over Europe again, but with particular virulence in France and Austria. Both nations quickly suppressed the rebels, but the need to concentrate on their own internal problems temporarily opened up the possibility for other revolutionary forces to act. The northern Italian regions of Lombardy and Venice, which for centuries had sought to retain independence from French and Austrian pressures on the one hand and the Papal States on the other, took advantage of the situation to declare war against Austria. Austria responded with heavy incursions into the disputed Italian territory. The future commandant of the Swiss Guard took part in the battles that ensued as an officer in the two papal divisions that the Holy Father had placed under General Durando to guard the northern frontier of the papal territories. It was in one of the battles of this campaign near the city of Vicenza that Meyer helped capture from the Austrians the very gun with which he would later be threatened in the rebellion outside the Quirinale Palace. In that same battle, four hundred Swiss fighting on behalf of the Papal States fell to superior forces but acquitted themselves so well that the Austrian command praised their courage in the peace negotiations. In October of 1848, Meyer was given the Order of St. Gregory by Pius IX for bravery under fire.

In mid-1848 as the battle was raging, however, Pius IX also had gone almost an entire year — he had accepted Martin Pfyffer's resignation in July 1847 — without a commander for the Swiss Guard. Providence or fate intervened at this point. The Swiss fighting for the Papal States in northern Italy were ordered by the king of Sardinia, an Italian ally, to attack the Austrians at another point. In their peace negotiation at Vicenza, however, they had promised not to return to battle against the Austrians for at least three months. A delegation, which included Meyer, went to explain to the pope why, in good conscience, they could not obey this order. Pius must have been impressed with the young Swiss officer because after Meyer departed to return to his unit the pope decided to send after him and ask if he would take on the command of the Swiss Guard provisionally, until relations with Lucerne could be regularized again. Little did Meyer realize as he spoke with Vatican officials about the post what a difficult job of reform he would face, to say nothing of the uprising in the piazza of the Quirinale which would occur within a few months.

Energetic and intelligent leader that he was, Meyer soon figured out that the widespread problems among the guards were a mix of bad policies that strained individual finances and the insubordinate attitudes that had grown up owing to failures in leadership. For instance, in the past, guards paid for their own uniforms out of their own monies and then were supposed to be reimbursed from a special fund controlled by the commandant. It not only placed the primary burden for maintaining uniforms on the young enlisted men, who were already living on the edge of poverty; it allowed for disputes with the commandant if it were suspected that he was holding back money, whether for good or bad reasons. Meyer seems to have found that the former commandants had not always had good motives, and he suggested to the pope that in a revised constitution the commandant should no longer be allowed such liberties. Also, he was surprised to find that the Swiss Guard, alone among all the papal forces, did not receive an automatic pay raise for years of service. As in most jobs, even those done in service to the Catholic Church, this basic lack of compensation for loyalty could not help but become a disincentive for good men to remain in the Guard, and it created problems as guards grew older and perhaps wished to marry and start a family. Meyer moved quickly to remedy all this as well as to instill the kind of military discipline that an officer with long experience among line troops expected.

It was providential that he did so because, within a few months, he and his men had to face the difficult task of controlling the revolutionary crowd outside of the Quirinale Palace. Though that episode was disturbing, to many people at the time it seemed to be merely one of the several upheavals that over recent years had temporarily displaced the pope and unsettled the political order without much changing the basic shape of Roman society. They and Meyer himself might have thought upon his return to the Holy City in mid-1849 that life would return to normal and continue much as it had since the late sixteenth century. The uprisings all over Europe in 1848, however, were not the end of a revolutionary period but the beginning of much larger social unrest. The French troops who restored papal rule in 1849 were the only real barrier between the Holy See and the growing Italian unification movement. When Pius IX rode back through the gates of Porta San Giovanni on April 12, 1850, neither he nor the Swiss guard who accompanied him — nor the fickle Roman people who welcomed him back enthusiastically — had any idea that within twenty years the pope's governance of the city of Rome, which had existed in one form or another for over a thousand years, would finally come to an end.

In the meantime, though, all good order was observed. Pius IX dubbed Meyer a knight for his shrewd handling of the situation at the Quirinale. The guards as a whole were awarded a medal for fidelity (*fidelitati*), in view of their steadfastness under very difficult circumstances. Pay levels were raised — always a morale booster — and special bonuses for length of service were offered at shorter intervals. Oddly, Pius IX took his time about permanently naming Meyer, who was still provisional commandant, to his post. Perhaps the recent troubles with his predecessors made the pope wary even about a man who had shown himself so competent in war and peace. Meyer took it all in stride, even when he lost a finger in an accident, which left him crippled for the rest of his life. More seriously, he suffered serious financial losses involving his property at home in Switzerland. He asked the pope for leave and upon his return reported on his financial situation to the pope, who immediately took steps to fix the problem. As a result, Meyer was finally able to marry and start a family. Despite some drawn-out intrigues on the part of the Pfyffers, which caused Meyer no little annoyance, the outcome seems to have never been in doubt, and he finally became permanent commandant in December of 1856. He did not remain long in the post that he had by then occupied "temporarily" for eight years. In 1860, he fell ill and died. His funeral was a lavish one, befitting the services he had performed at a crucial moment, and his body received a final blessing from Pius IX.

The End of the Papal States

Pius moved quickly to name a much-decorated forty-five-year-old man to replace Meyer. Albert von Sonnenberg had served with distinction as a contract soldier in various armies from those of Naples and the Two Sicilies to the forces of the Swiss Catholic cantons during the very brief war (twenty-seven days) between Swiss Catholics and Protestants known as the *Sonderbundskrieg* of 1847. Von Sonnenberg was immediately thrown into the most challenging situation the Holy See had ever faced, and he was fortunate that his predecessor had bequeathed to him a well-ordered contingent of men. From 1860 to 1870 the various political bits and pieces that for centuries had kept the Italian peninsula in a fragmented and decentralized condition began to be united under the leadership of King Victor Emmanuel of the House of Savoy in northern Italy. Just one sign of how odd a task this was is that the future king did not even speak Italian easily. Like most Italians until long after unification, he spoke a regional dialect; and like many of them he felt stronger ties to a region (a phenomenon known as *campanilismo* in Italian, from the word that refers to the local church tower — *campanile*) than he did to the vague geographic entity Italy.[10] Yet Italian unification seemed inevitable if Italy was not to remain a mosaic of small squabbling jurisdictions, as was still the case in Germany as well.

Victor Emmanuel swiftly took possession of several northern Italian principalities including parts of the Papal States. His diplomats convinced France that such moves were necessary to check France's own arch-rival at the time, Austria. French troops still guaranteed the independence of Rome itself, but it is never a good thing when a state must rely on another's army for independence. It was only a matter of time before circumstances made it impossible for France to continue protecting Rome. Though Victor Emmanuel and his deputies approached Rome with great caution, not wanting to provoke any of the major European powers or to raise Catholic sentiment against their steady expansion, it was clear that for many reasons, both practical and symbolic, only Rome, with its incomparably rich history, could be the capital of the new Italian kingdom.

For most people, even for most Catholics, the last days of the Papal States — which led finally to the unification of Italy as a modern nation — are not a milestone to be lamented. The subsequent history of the papacy has been such that the pope and the Vatican have actually gained in worldwide moral stature with the separation of the tiny Vatican City State from its long-held territories across the center of the Italian peninsula. But this happy result for all parties should not obscure some real fears that existed at the time. In Continental Europe, relations between Church and State had been rocky, especially where fiery revolutionaries believed that to create democracies the Church had to be destroyed. Eventually, concordats and other special legislation had to be developed in some instances to protect churches from political intrusions.

The papal territories had existed for almost as long as the Roman Empire, and within that time had no small number of achievements to its credit, as the art and architecture of the modern city of Rome can still attest. Italian unification, like the German unification that happened around the same time, had to come, but the Papal States presented a special problem and required unproven new arrangements before unification could be seen as the blessing it became.

It also required a military and political shift. As odd as it may seem today, until 1870 the pope was the ruler of both an earthly realm and a spiritual realm, and like other terrestrial rulers he had a political and economic administration, and even an army.[11] One of Italy's great statesmen of the period of unification, Camillo Cavour, slowly persuaded the French, the main outside ally of the papal forces, to align themselves with the growing Italian kingdom against Austria, a major power dominant in Venice and the region around Milan known as Lombardy. During the 1850s, after several military defeats, Austria abandoned Lombardy. And the growing political momentum encouraged voters in Tuscany and several other important northern Italian regions to choose to join in the movement for unity and independence, which still had some distance to go, especially with regard to the Papal States and the Kingdom of the Two Sicilies.

A two-front movement began. The northern allies under Sardinian leadership took over all of the Papal States, including the Marches and Umbria, except for Rome itself. The famous Italian general Giuseppe Garibaldi with his Thousand Men (*Mille*) occupied Sicily and Naples in the south. Populations in all those regions voted in large numbers, though with some irregularities and pressure, to join together in the creation of Italy. Austria, under attack from Prussia (allied with the Italians), was forced to give up Venice. All that remained for the final unification of the peninsula was the city that of historical necessity seemed to have to become the capital of the new Italian nation: what pagans and Christians alike call the Eternal City, Rome itself.

The capture of Rome required delicate international diplomacy before the final military assault. The French under Napoleon III put troops there, and anyone who attacked Rome risked provoking France. The Italian king Victor Emmanuel, Garibaldi, and others tried to reassure France and the pope, and French troops began to be withdrawn. But the assurances given — even had they been sincere (they were not) — could not possibly hold, and the first opportunity showed as much. In 1870, war broke out between the French and the Prussians. The French had to withdraw all troops from Italy to defend themselves at home; Rome immediately became vulnerable to attack. It was quickly occupied only six days after the Battle of Sedan, a decisive engagement near the border between France and Belgium on September 20, 1870. Pope Pius IX famously became "prisoner of the Vatican," which is to say of the Leonine City, the tiny territory that still belongs to the Holy See. The Vatican was voted special privileges by the Italian Parliament in 1871, but Pius refused to accept them. Relations remained unsettled until the 1929 Lateran Treaty, when Italy and the Holy See entered into a concordat that, with a few modifications, is the same relationship the two entities have today.

The Swiss were deeply involved in this major shift in the status of the pope as a temporal as well as a spiritual ruler. All around the Catholic world, young men volunteered in defense of the Papal States: Switzerland, Ireland, Austria, France, Belgium, and other states saw young men set off to join the Papal Zouaves, which were commanded by a Swiss colonel.

Meanwhile the Swiss guards proper, like Pius IX, continued their usual activities despite the rising tides around them. Pius was an unflappable man, sometimes bordering on the obsessive, and he received visitors and carried out his traditional functions as if nothing were happening. Indeed, partly as a way to bolster his position, in 1864 Pius issued a stern encyclical, *Quanta Cura,* condemning modernism, which was accompanied by the notorious Syllabus of Errors, a list of forbidden practices including freedom of speech, press, and religion, and the separation of Church and State. It also rejected suggestions that the pope should give up temporal rule and that "the Roman Pontiff can and should reconcile himself to progress, liberalism, and modern civilization." All such views were classified by Pius as *deliramenta,* roughly delirium. Defenders of the pope rightly point out that these statements were made in the context of immediate political pressure and do not even accord with some of Pius IX's own earlier practices.

That same year the Italians signed the so-called September Treaty with France, by which they promised not to invade the Papal States. Modern histories often underscore the desperate resistance of the pope and the Papal States at the time; they less often point out the bad faith and double-dealing that the Italian kingdom practiced repeatedly and quite consciously during the 1860s. Even the final assault on Rome by Italian forces was defended by the royal officials as merely an effort to keep down "disorder," a frequent plea of conquerors. By 1866, the Italians had defeated Austria at Königgrätz, and Vienna had to concede Venice and its territories to the new Italian kingdom. With the House of Savoy's troops closing in from the north and Garibaldi's Redshirts moving up from the south, Pius announced the convening of an ecumenical council that would later come to be known as Vatican I. At that gathering of many of the world's bishops, he pressed for a declaration of papal infallibility. Catholics had always believed that an infallible authority of a kind existed in the Church ("the gates of Hell shall not prevail") without ever really spelling out how it was to be understood. Pius pushed hard, but the assembled bishops qualified the infallibility as pertaining only to faith and morals, and only on those occasions when the pope speaks formally *ex cathedra,* from his chair as successor of Peter. (In the more than 150 years since the proclamation, the pope has only used the power twice — each time to make a proclamation about the Virgin Mary, never on any other subject.) In any event, papal infallibility did little to stop the advance of the Italian king. Papal infallibility was voted on July 18, 1870; on September 20, the Italian forces breached the walls of Rome near Porta Pia, and the Papal States, except for Vatican City and the extraterritorial churches in the city of Rome, ceased to exist.

The Swiss and the "Prisoner of the Vatican"

The Swiss guards played as brave a part as they could in these massive historical developments. In 1867, Swiss Guard Commandant von Sonnenberg was appointed by General Hermann von Kanzler, a Swiss military man and the pope's overall commander, to his general staff, and served simultaneously with his men in the "Roman Legion" of the papal troops. As the enemy under the leadership of Giuseppe Garibaldi advanced, Swiss guards were put on constant alert to keep an eye on certain points around the Vatican. Instead of their customary halberds, they were issued more useful swords and other real weapons. Meanwhile, terror tactics were deployed within the city by sympathizers with the national cause. Bombs went off in barracks and commissaries. A group of Swiss officers were wounded when someone threw a bomb at them in Piazza Colonna. One group of saboteurs very nearly blew up the stores of gunpowder in the papal fortress of Castel Sant'Angelo in Rome. It was fortunate they failed, because there was enough explosive power in the old castle to have caused massive destruction over a good portion of the Vatican as we know it today. The Swiss, the papal forces, and some two thousand French troops were able to turn back Garibaldi's advance on November 4, 1867, causing fourteen hundred deaths and perhaps another thousand wounded. The pope later commended the entire Swiss Guard for bravery under fire and presented all of them with a medal for faith and virtue (*fidei et virtuti*). But it was only a temporary victory.

The next year Pius announced the forthcoming council, which meant that the Swiss would have to manage security issues for the pope and the council fathers on top of the very real military role they now played. And in the meantime, Pius did not slacken the pace of his usual visits and consultations with foreign dignitaries. Nor did he fail to celebrate his fiftieth anniversary as a priest in 1869 (the Swiss received two barrels of wine from him for the occasion). But the fateful year 1870 soon arrived. It was something of a historical irony that the situation of the modern papacy changed forever on two consecutive days. On July 18, 1870, papal infallibility was proclaimed by the bishops assembled in St. Peter's Basilica. The very next day Prussia and France went to war, making it impossible for French troops to remain in Rome in numbers sufficient to keep the surrounding Italian troops at bay. The pope still had about ten thousand men of various backgrounds under the command of General Kanzler. Commandant von Sonnenberg asked for Remington rifles and sufficient ammunition for all 120 of his men. One of the last services they were able to perform before the pope was besieged in the Vatican was to go with him on September 19 to the Sacred Stairs (*Scala Santa*) near the basilica of St. John Lateran and pray. The following day, after five hours of cannon fire, a breach was opened at Porta Pia in northeastern Rome, and the invaders took possession of the city.

Pius IX knew by this point that his troops could not withstand the assault. He ordered them to resist only until a breach opened in the city wall and then to surrender so as to minimize casualties. General Kanzler had white flags raised at various places at the appointed times. The Italian invaders, with only one unfortunate exception (a continued and highly destructive bombardment of the area called Trastevere), ceased fire as ordered by their own General Cadorna. Both sides showed honor to one another in the terms of surrender. The Swiss guards were called to the Vatican along with many Church officials, military commanders, and members of the diplomatic corps, where they stood guard over the proceedings. Pius spoke with many present and then released them with commendations for those who fought on his behalf. The new Italian government of the city allowed the foreigners to leave. Before they did so, however, they assembled all together one last time in St. Peter's Square, where they sang songs, shouted support for the papal cause, and received a final blessing from the pope.

The Swiss and a few other special papal forces remained behind. The new circumstances in Italy altered their papal service within the Vatican. The Italian government wanted as good relations with the Vatican as possible for several reasons. First, Victor Emmanuel was a Catholic and did not relish any unnecessary tension with the Church. In fact, like many Italians, he was quite favorable toward the pope except for the continuation of papal political power in central Italy. Also, the king wished to defuse potential charges by foreign powers that he had subordinated the Church to the State, or that he held the pope a prisoner. The new regime quickly moved to pass "the law of guarantees," and the king signed the legislation on May 13, 1871. In essence, these guarantees made special provisions for the pope and the Church. They declared the pope's person "sacred and inviolable," a status similar to that of the king. In accord with the views of Count Camillo Cavour, the royal prime minister, the Catholic Church was to be "a free Church within a free State." Vatican City along with St. John Lateran (the pope's basilica as bishop of Rome), Castel Gandolfo, and other church holdings such as museums and libraries were declared papal property exempt from taxation and the jurisdiction of the Italian government. In fact, the government offered the pope more than three million lire a year tax-free for his expenses.[12]

Pius IX rejected all this, however, and excommunicated all those involved in the new Italian government from the king down. Thus began a period in which the pope regarded himself as a "prisoner of the Vatican," a self-imposed restriction since he would have been free to travel around the country had he wished. Pius called upon Catholics abroad to come to Italy and retake the papal territories on his behalf. But by this point it seemed to most people that the question of Italian unity had finally been settled. Germany was undergoing a similar unification of its equally long-fragmented territory. Modern conditions seemed to require larger, more integrated areas to create stability and order. No serious movement to reconquer the Papal States arose. As a result, the pope and his Swiss guards were to spend several decades in the late nineteenth and early twentieth centuries exclusively within the perimeter of Vatican City.

During the early days of this period in particular, the Swiss guards carried guns openly around the Vatican in order to be ready for any eventuality. When they were performing guard duty close to the pope himself, however, they reverted to their traditional halberds. Under the circumstances, large public celebrations involving the pope were now sharply reduced, and the guards therefore had fewer ceremonial responsibilities. All the Swiss now drew extended watch duty in light of the uncertainty about what the Italian government might do next. The Swiss contingent at the Quirinale Palace was ordered back to the Vatican to help with the heavier schedule. Within a short time, Victor Emmanuel moved his court from Florence to Rome and took up residence at the Quirinale, to the great annoyance of the pope.

The uncertainty of the situation in Rome along with steep inflation and renewed opposition back in Switzerland to paid military service abroad began to take a toll on recruiting efforts for new Swiss guards. A year after the Italians captured the Holy City, the number of guards had fallen to seventy-six. Fortunately, fifteen new recruits quickly turned up, a dozen from the Valais and three from the traditional inner Swiss Catholic cantons.[13] But bad habits started to creep into the guards, probably because of the constant pressure within the Leonine City. Military discipline, including cleanliness — one of Commandant von Sonnenberg's obsessions — sharply declined. Guards started to show up and perform their watches smoking pipes or cigars. All smoking had to be prohibited outside of certain areas. Harsh punishments were imposed for infractions of the commandant's orders. Tempers seemed on edge in general, perhaps owing to the near state of siege within the Vatican. Conditions seem to have provoked rebellion, ostensibly over financial matters. Things came to a head with the death of Pius IX (February 7, 1878) and the election of the new pope Leo XIII (February 20, 1878). The guards were usually given special bonuses on such occasions and expected for some reason much more than the usual payments. When these were not forthcoming, over forty guards resigned. Leo partly blamed von Sonnenberg for this, though the commandant was easily able to recruit young men to fill the openings. With the accession of the new pope, Commandant von Sonnenberg decided to retire and the following September departed for Nice, where he died in 1883.

The Close of the Nineteenth Century

For the rest of the nineteenth century, the Swiss guards were led by Louis Martin de Courten, of the Valais, not from Lucerne, the traditional home of Swiss commanders. De Courten was from a long line of Swiss military men and had served alongside former Swiss commandant Franz Leopold Meyer von Schauensee in the notorious battle at Vicenza, mentioned earlier. There he had been hit by a bullet but by sheer luck remained uninjured when it ricocheted off one of his buckles. The future commandant had served for ten years as head of the pope's foreign carabinieri and as such dealt with all sorts of disorders in the Papal States, including gangs of bandits and murderers. When the Italian forces had breached Porta Pia on September 20, 1870, de Courten was in charge of the papal artillery that opposed them from Piazza San Bernardino, the small square between the American church of Santa Susanna and the church of Santa Maria della Vittoria, which houses Bernini's famous statue *The Ecstasy of St. Teresa*. The piazza lay on the direct route between Porta Pia and the Quirinale Palace, and de Courten and his men were barely able to escape capture and make their way back to the Vatican. There he departed with the ten thousand foreign troops who were allowed to leave the city and went home, he thought, to a quiet life in the Swiss town of Siders.

His retirement came to an end eight years later when the pope asked him to return to Rome as the commander of his Swiss Guard. In his first speech to his men, de Courten reminded them of the high service to which they had been called and the need for them to devote themselves wholly to that service: "Every Catholic country envies Switzerland because of this great honor," he told them. His time as head of the guards, however, passed in relative quiet as the situation in the new Italy settled into routine. De Courten was highly skilled in balancing two much needed qualities during the period. On the one hand, he maintained the strictest military discipline, demanding the most careful observance of all orders and regulations. He requested and received 120 Remington rifles and a year's worth of ammunition for his men and then drilled them in an open space near the Belvedere so that they would be in a condition to protect the pope should relations with the Italian monarchy worsen. On the other hand, he took very good care of all the needs of his men. He exerted himself to improve their living conditions, especially in taking hygienic measures against the fevers that often struck foreigners in Rome. De Courten also seems to have understood the need for keeping up morale in the relatively cramped space of Vatican City. He founded a musical band of guards, who played for visiting groups, and he set up a library where the men could read during their free time. Abstemious himself, de Courten allowed a fair amount of good-natured wine drinking at celebrations, which also served to keep the men happy.

His health began to fail in 1900, just as the new century was beginning, but de Courten stayed on in order to make sure that the Jubilee Year was properly handled. He retired on June 1, 1901, at the age of sixty-five, much praised for his productive life and much decorated by the pope. He took up residence on a farm belonging to his wife near Nancy in what is today eastern France, expecting to live out the few years remaining to him in peace. In

1935, he was still alive and received congratulations from Pius XI on the occasion of his hundredth birthday. It was only after his wife passed away that his age seems finally to have caught up with him. De Courten died in March of 1939 at the age of 104, a living bridge between the age of European revolutions in the first half of the nineteenth century and the age of dictatorships, which, in that year, took a serious turn with the outbreak of World War II and which would afflict the Church and the world for most of the twentieth century.

Chapter Seven

The Guard during the Two World Wars and the German Occupation of Rome

THE TWENTIETH CENTURY brought large and rapid changes in the functioning of the papacy. The sweeping nature of these developments is immediately evident in a simple glance at the two very different figures who occupied the chair of Peter at the beginning and the end of the century. In 1900, Leo XIII, though a progressive and highly intellectual man — indeed, one of the first architects of what would later become known as modern Catholic social teaching — still was thought of, and even regarded himself, as a "prisoner of the Vatican." Unresolved questions with the Italian monarchy about territorial rights and jurisdiction meant that no pope had set foot outside the precincts of the old Leonine City since 1870. And that would remain the case until 1929, ending a period of almost sixty years during which the activities of the Vatican were mostly conducted inside its own walls. By 2000, however, Leo's counterpart, John Paul II, was a world figure, not only because of the globe-trotting he had done to evangelize and promote peace and justice on every continent. The pope on the eve of the new Christian millennium exercised great moral authority and may even have been the most respected public figure then alive for Catholics and non-Catholics alike. That authority grew in large part from the popes' gradual emergence from being Italian princes of a sort toward their status as purely spiritual figures carrying out a mission carefully crafted to meet modern needs. Such large-scale institutional evolution could not help but substantially change a corps of men as close to the day-to-day life of the pope as the Swiss Guard.

The century began calmly enough for the guards, and they played various roles with honor and distinction. Many of these functions were longstanding; some were quite unprecedented. For instance, in 1903, the year of his twenty-fifth anniversary, Leo XIII decided one fitting way to celebrate the occasion would be to hold a dinner for one thousand of Rome's poor within the Vatican. The guards kept order at the event — and also provided the entertainment: the Swiss Guard band played for an audience who had certainly never had such a dinner and performance dedicated to them before. They also provided traditional color, as many observers noted, at the more public events for the anniversary when the whole of Rome celebrated with the aging pontiff, lighting bonfires in a row seven miles long, which were visible from the pope's apartments. When Leo died and the conclave to elect his successor began, journalists remarked on the doubling of the Swiss security forces and both the efficiency and effectiveness of their measures to make sure that the cardinals would be isolated from any outside interference. As one journalist wrote at the time: "The complicated blockade is worked with remarkable smoothness, as if a conclave were a frequent event for which the Vatican was constantly drilled."[1]

The new pope, Pius X (Giuseppe Melchiorre Sarto), was a man of very simple background and piety, so much so that he would be declared a saint within a few years of his death. Early in his papacy Pius X made it clear that he felt uncomfortable having to travel with bodyguards and that he thought armed men somewhat out of place in the Holy See. Shortly after his election, the Palatine Guards — one of the five Vatican security forces that existed at the time — got into an uproar over internal tensions. This unrest deepened Pius X's unease about his armed escorts. Then, in 1912, a virtual revolt arose among the Swiss guards over the strict military training that had been introduced by their commandant,

Jules Repond, who had been appointed two years earlier. Repond was a career military man and believed that the guards should be a real military force. His critics accused him of having turned the Vatican into a *place des armes*. Given that World War I was just around the corner and that the guards would indeed play an important military role in World War II, he was not entirely wrong in believing that the Swiss Guard should be ready for anything. But at the time, his reintroduction of military training and modern weapons seemed out of place both to his men and to the authorities in the Holy See.

Matters came to a head in the summer heat of July 1912. Repond had been making the guards do strenuous bayonet training, shooting on a firing range, and even climbing over rooftops with ropes in preparation for a possible assault on the Holy City. In mid-July, a kind of "mutiny" occurred when some men refused to do patrols. They received sentences of two months in prison. The situation was so precarious that the authorities had to lock up all weapons in the Swiss armory, and Repond armed himself against possible personal attacks. A group of guards presented a list of grievances to Cardinal Merry del Val, then Vatican secretary of state. They had six demands:

1. The dismissal of Jules Repond
2. An increase in the number of guards from eighty to one hundred, which would allow for more days off each week
3. Election of officers by the guards themselves
4. No restrictions on the visiting of Roman stores and wine shops by guards
5. Cessation of the bayonet drills, target practice, and rooftop exercises, and a return to the guards' traditional roles
6. No punishment for anyone involved in the current protest

Naturally this was far more than the cardinal or any responsible official could ever allow without inviting further insubordination.

In fact, Merry del Val expelled the ringleaders and only narrowly averted the abolition of the guards by Pius X, who initially ordered precisely that but was later persuaded to relent. Some figures in the Vatican suggested that perhaps it was time to "internationalize" the Swiss Guard by recruiting volunteers from the entire Catholic world, as had been done during the second half of the nineteenth century with the Papal Zouaves.

World War I and Two Swiss Anniversaries

The Swiss, however, seemed to many other people in the Vatican to be an integral part of the Holy See's operations and a link with tradition that should not be broken. Once this incident quieted down, they returned to their usual tasks. But World War I, as would be the case later to an even greater degree in the Second World War, had serious effects within the Vatican. Two events in rapid succession in the summer of 1914 even led to a brief period in which the guards were unable to carry out their duties. The war broke out in July of that year, and Switzerland immediately requested and received permission from the pope for fifty of the Swiss guards to return home for active national duty. The next month Pius X died, and the number of Swiss guards in Rome was not adequate for the management of the funeral and the conclave to elect a successor. An odd arrangement was put in place for only about a month, which solved the problem: seminarians from Austria, Bohemia, Germany, Hungary, and Luxemburg volunteered as "Swiss" guards throughout the conclave. When it was all over, Repond started recruiting more widely in Switzerland and brought a number of French-speaking guards to Rome. He thus managed to weather his second crisis within two years. His period of command continued to be marked by strict discipline and undeniable improvements in certain aspects of the guards' work, but his strong personality inevitably brought him into conflict with Vatican superiors and the other papal military forces. He retired early from the service in 1921.

At the 1922 conclave that elected Pius XI, the guards apprehended and ejected a photographer who had wormed his way into the Sistine Chapel where the cardinals were conducting sacred business. The Swiss often wore modern uniforms at the time modeled on the French or the Prussian army as fashions might dictate, and they carried the Mauser rifles Jules Repond had obtained for them. But Repond had also taken a great interest in historic Swiss guard uniforms and even wrote a book on the subject.[2] On special ceremonial occasions, they began to wear Renaissance garb that Repond had re-created by studying the frescoes of the artist Raphael that showed the Swiss Guard attending the pope in the sixteenth century. As might be expected, these injected notable new color into Vatican events. At the 1924 consistory that appointed new cardinals, the guards were described as "looking almost unreal in their multicolored uniforms, steel breastplates, and plumed helmets, and carrying serpentine swords appearing like tongues of flame on their shoulders."[3]

The guards had celebrated their four hundredth anniversary in 1906 in a relatively quiet way. But in 1927, under Commandant Alois Hirschbühl, a Swiss nobleman, they took special pride in commemorating the four hundredth anniversary of the deaths of their 147 predecessors who had fallen in the 1527 sack of Rome. A monumental fountain with the figure of Kaspar Röist, the Swiss commandant who had given his life in defense of Clement VII, was unveiled and dedicated by Pius XI in the courtyard formed by the Swiss barracks.

As events soon proved, the renewed confidence in the guards was not merely ceremonial. When the Lateran Treaty was signed in 1929, regularizing the relationship between the Holy See and the Italian government, one of the ways in which the new relationship was symbolized was a shift in the public face of the Holy See. The Portone di Bronzo, the large brass doorway to the right of St. Peter's, was now wide open during daytime hours and conspicuously manned by the Swiss guards. During the formal visit by Mussolini to exchange copies of the treaty, Italian carabinieri withdrew from the perimeter of the Holy City and were replaced by Swiss carrying rifles, a symbol of the Vatican's new status. The Swiss were also now evident at all the entrances to the Vatican as they had not been during the years when the popes felt as if they were "prisoners" in Rome. They controlled access to the little over one hundred acres that were part of what had long been called the Leonine City, meaning roughly the area that since Pope Leo X had been regarded as the core of the papal buildings and grounds. In the years immediately following this opening up to the Italian state, the Vatican modernized rapidly, developing a train station, radio towers, and other trappings of technological progress. But the Holy See maintained, with Swiss help, the deep quiet within the Vatican complex, especially in its gardens, which for centuries had been one of its most charming dimensions.

The New Legal Situation

The basic legal framework under which the Vatican and the Swiss Guard operated in Rome from the late 1920s until after 1945 was laid out by the 1929 concordat that Pius XI signed with Benito Mussolini's government. It is important to understand what a "concordat" is and is not in order to appraise this arrangement properly and to appreciate how it affected the relationship between the Vatican and the Italian state, and later between the Holy See and the German occupiers of Rome. A concordat is an agreement with a secular government about relations between the state and the Catholic Church. It is not a statement about or endorsement of the moral behavior of that state. The whole phenomenon of concordats emerged as European states radically secularized themselves after the French Revolution (1789); it is no surprise that the first concordat (with France) signed by the Vatican came in 1801 after negotiations with Napoleon. As we have already seen, Napoleon, while still a general, had kidnapped Pius VI from Rome in 1798 (the pope died in captivity in France the following year). And in spite of the concordat, Napoleon as emperor also held Pius VII captive from 1805 to 1809. Clearly, a concordat might help organize relations and spell out respective spheres of competency — and thereby assist the operations of the Church — but if a secular state with adequate armed forces decided to break such an agreement, there was not much the Church could do about it.

The Catholic Church under several popes signed more than thirty concordats with various countries during the nineteenth century.[4] For the most part, these sought to safeguard essential Church functions such as free appointment of bishops, liberty for Catholic Action (an umbrella organization consisting of various Catholic social groups), and legal standing for the Church to conduct marriages. While all these foreign agreements seemed to work reasonably well, the relationship to the new Italian kingdom remained unsettled after the occupation of Rome by the army of the Italian king. Successive popes refused to recognize the secular jurisdiction, and what was called the "Roman Question" remained open. Italy had proposed a Law of Guarantees, but the Holy See rejected the idea as making the Church dependent on the Italian state. At the same time, it became clear, even within the Vatican, that there was no going back to the days when the Holy See ruled a wide swath of land across the center of the Italian peninsula or even Rome herself. The Roman Question was a matter of how the Holy See would fit in — and be indemnified by — the new Italian nation.

During the Versailles peace talks after World War I, Pope Benedict XV sent a cardinal, Bonaventura Cerretti, to discuss the Vatican's position with then Italian prime minister Vittorio Emmanuele Orlando. An American bishop, Francis C. Kelley, who was a highly skilled diplomat, was the intermediary who arranged the discussions. But any real action had to wait for a new pope, Pius XI, a vigorous and active man (he had been an enthusiastic mountain climber before he became pope) and a new prime minister, Mussolini, both of whom came to power in 1922. It is clear that Pius XI was eager from the very start of his papacy to reach a settlement with Italy, and Mussolini, too, wanted an agreement that would bolster his position. In 1924, the pope signed a concordat with Bavaria and began negotiations with Prussia, followed by concordats with Latvia, Poland, Romania, Lithuania, and Portugal.[5] He seems to have believed strongly the old adage "governments pass away, documents stay."

On the one hand, negotiations with Mussolini were facilitated by the fact that members of the Catholic party in Italy, the Partito Popolare, were included in the prime minister's cabinet. A Jesuit, Pietro Tacchi Venturi, was even a member of the Fascist Party itself and acted as a go-between. On the other hand, Mussolini was a professed socialist and an open and virulent opponent of Christianity, which he had denounced in print and in speeches many times. But Il Duce was a shrewd politician and student of history. He believed — and later even tried to convince Hitler — that direct confrontation with the Church throughout history inevitably led to political defeat. So he pursued a different strategy, taking steps to co-opt the Church: he allowed crucifixes in schools and courts, ordered religious instruction in public schools, muzzled anticlericalism, recognized Catholic universities, attended religious ceremonies, and helped rebuild damaged churches. To be sure, Mussolini did all this for pragmatic political gain, but pragmatism for him meant acknowledging the truth: "We are a Catholic nation not only because the vast majority of our people is Catholic, but because Catholicism is inseparable from our history."[6]

Over the next few years the relationship between the Church and the Italian state had its ups and downs, and several currents within Mussolini's Fascist Party opposed any concessions to the Holy See. But the negotiations moved forward, and on February 11, 1929, the two sides signed the Lateran Agreement, which spelled out a harmonious relationship that included recognition of Catholicism as the sole official religion and also compensated the Vatican for loss of certain territories. It also imposed political neutrality on the Vatican, however, which was to be "extraneous to all temporal disputes between states," a clause that would pose no little difficulty during World War II and beyond. The two parties also signed a formal concordat that, like those with other nations, spelled out relations on broader topics. Basic Catholic morality shaped state institutions, and the Church had the right to conduct legal marriages. In a sort of compensation, the Church would not allow clerics to be involved in political parties or politics. The Vatican was so confident of these arrangements that, when Mussolini made anticlerical speeches soon after, it barely noticed them and knew they would not affect the agreements. Criticism arose on both the Fascist and Catholic sides — in addition to specific details, each feared identification with the other — but there was no undoing this resolution of a problem that had persisted for more than half a century.

The Swiss under the Concordat

For the Swiss Guard, all this had an immediate legal impact. Since the Roman Question now seemed resolved and the Holy See's status appeared to be guaranteed by the Italian monarchy, which wholly surrounded the territories controlled by the Church, the Swiss Federal Council formally declared a few days later, "Henceforth the Papal Guard cannot be considered a foreign armed force as described in article 94 of the military penal code, because the troops are simply a police force. Therefore, any man may join the service, as at present, without authorization from the Federal Council."[7] Ironically, as was to appear quite shortly, this was a highly optimistic assessment of the situation, and within fifteen years the Vatican would face one of the most formidable threats ever when Nazi Germany occupied Rome. For the moment, it was true that Mussolini had personally changed Church-State relations substantially for the better, despite his totalitarianism (a term he invented). Yet as has been the case throughout history, no one man, however powerful, can guarantee political arrangements for very long, even assuming he continues in office. Mussolini was no exception. His alliance with Hitler, after the latter came to power in 1933, put him directly at odds with both the Holy See and the Western Allies. Though he survived throughout the 1930s unscathed, the outbreak of World War II would lead to Mussolini's death and great complications for the Vatican and for the Swiss guards in its defense.

Things came to a head in 1943. By that point, the Axis powers were clearly losing the war, and Mussolini's grip on his own Fascist Party in Italy was coming to an end. On July 19, Allied B-17s and B-24s dropped the first bombs on Rome herself, which up until then, unlike other European cities, had been spared. They encountered no resistance — not a single fighter plane — from the Italian Air Force. The armed forces and the government were virtually bankrupt. King Vittorio Emmanuele III had probably decided before that July day that Mussolini had to go. But the attack gave him the opportunity he needed to act. Within the week, a Fascist congress had voted no confidence, and in a meeting with the king, Mussolini was arrested and taken in an ambulance out of Rome. Vittorio Emmanuele named Marshal Pietro Badoglio as the new prime minister. Back in Germany, Adolf Hitler regarded all this as sheer betrayal and expected that, if he did not do something, the Badoglio government would surrender to the Allies (a step Badoglio immediately began planning, as the records show), thereby virtually assuring the swift demise of Nazi Germany. After carefully calibrating the various factors, Hitler moved a large number of troops into Italy, and, by September 11, Rome was occupied by German forces.

The situation after the German arrival in 1943 was especially complicated legally. In theory, the Fascist government remained in power, though the king, Badoglio, and his ministers had fled. In theory, the 1929 concordat with the government of Italy remained in effect. That meant that the papal holdings designated as "extraterritorial" by the Italian government stayed under the jurisdiction of the Holy See as before. In reality, the nature of the Italian government had become less clear; and the forces that now ruled Rome were a dangerous combination of Italian Fascist goons and German Nazi occupation troops. These complexities had already given rise to some differences of opinion among the Swiss guards, as Italian intelligence services noted (they kept a close eye on the guards and the diplomats accredited to the Vatican for signs of resistance). But the predominant tone among the guards seems to have been rather vocal opposition to the Axis powers since as early as 1940 the Italian government had put pressure on the Vatican to forbid the Swiss from speaking about the war and politics.[8] Pius XII had also ordered the Swiss guards not to put up resistance in case of a Nazi invasion of the Vatican proper, but this went so contrary to instinct that the commandant, Heinrich Pfyffer von Altishofen, took an extraordinary step: he "demanded to see the order in writing."[9]

The German Occupation of Rome

Oddly, by the time that the Nazi *Wehrmacht* arrived in Rome in September 1943, the Vatican was commonly regarded in Europe as an active and substantial political entity again, probably owing to the freedom it enjoyed under the concordat. One anecdote from the period suggests precisely how large a public impression the pope and his little city-state had made. The young German soldiers who patrolled the streets outside the Holy City would sometimes stop and talk with the German-speaking Swiss. On one occasion, the Germans expressed their surprise that the Vatican was defended only by its traditional walls, a bit of barbed wire strung along the tops, and the few Swiss and Palatine guards who patrolled the perimeter carrying rifles. A Swiss guard later recorded: "We were particularly amused in talking with some of the German soldiers to learn they expected to encounter an air force and mechanized garrison in the Vatican."[10] Despite the lack of military resistance, the *Wehrmacht* was very careful — out of propaganda considerations — not to give the impression that it was threatening or planning to invade the Vatican. In fact, however, they mined the bridges leading to the papal enclave, probably in case they needed to prevent people from seeking asylum there. But the German troops stationed around the Vatican, despite justified fears, were careful never to infringe on papal territory.

They did, however, infringe on the more easygoing public presence of the Swiss. Unlike the period from 1929 to 1943, when relations with the Italian state, though not ideal, had made the border between the Holy See and Italy less tense, the presence of a threatening army had put a damper on daily operations. Beginning in 1943, the Vatican went back to its pre-1929 habits of conducting few events in public places, not even in St. Peter's Square. It was not until two years after the war, in 1946, that the Swiss guards were able to hold public swearing-in ceremonies again, by which time Allied military commanders were prominently situated among the distinguished visitors.

On Friday, September 10, 1943, shortly after Nazi forces had moved into Rome, an American woman living in the city with long experience in Italy recorded some extraordinary facts in her diary:

> By midday St. Peter's was shut. When, in the memory of man, had it been shut in the daytime? Still, of course it was wise. If a panic-stricken crowd had rushed into it for protection, the situation might well have become complicated. It looked very desolate. The same with the Vatican City: Porta Santa Anna [*sic*] was hermetically closed. At the Arco delle Campane [Arch of Bells] gate a Swiss with businesslike rifle and bayonet, instead of his medieval pike, guarded the entrance; in like manner there was one at the closed Portone di Bronzo. Palatine Guard reinforced the Swiss, who are not very numerous.[11]

It caused her to reflect on some of the other historical disasters that had befallen the Eternal City over its long existence: "[Robert] Guiscard's Normans wrecking that neighbourhood in

1084, and [the duke of] Bourbon's Lutheran hordes in 1527, were after all, not so very unlike Hitler's Huns riding in on their tanks and lorries, driving the defeated Romans before them as they went."

She had astutely noticed, however, some difference in this latest crisis, which had complicated the position of the Swiss guards. To begin with, the political situation in occupied Rome was a delicate one. The Swiss and the Holy See by this point had had ample experience in patrolling the borders of the tiny Vatican City State in order to maintain what independence they could from potentially hostile secular rulers. But the Nazi occupation ratcheted up the external threat beyond anything the Vatican had seen in almost three-quarters of a century. Though the Swiss and other Vatican forces were patrolling with firearms, they could not realistically be expected to withstand any serious German assault. The Germans desperately wanted to avoid that kind of confrontation. By late 1943, Allied forces had invaded southern Italy and were slowly making their way up the Italian peninsula. The Nazi propaganda machine did everything it could to portray its behavior toward the Vatican as actually protecting the pope from the disorder in Italy following Mussolini's expulsion as head of government some months earlier. Nazi sources claimed that the Vatican's properties remained unmolested and that it had free channels of communication with the outside world.

This was technically true, though the Germans would soon block all mail in and out of the Vatican, and also presented a carefully calculated threat. In fact, within days, a plane dropped four bombs across Vatican City. Investigations showed that the bombs were manufactured by the British, but almost everyone believed that the Germans, who had captured large numbers of such bombs during their military campaigns, had dropped them from one of their own planes either as a warning or as a propaganda ploy. In light of such possibilities, the Vatican's semiofficial newspaper, *L'Osservatore Romano,* made a point of communicating precise details about the situation to the rest of the world. As it said in one of its dispatches:

> Many rumors have been spread regarding conditions in the Vatican City and the person of the Holy Father, since the German occupation of Rome. As we have already stated, from the afternoon of September 13th, German soldiers have been posted in Piazza San Pietro, in Italian territory, outside the boundaries of the Vatican City. This action was preceded by a telephone call from the Italian Command of the City of Rome to the Governor of the Vatican City, who gave notice to the authorities. Two Vatican officials were directed to present themselves at the time appointed, 4 p.m., at the boundary line of the Vatican City to make sure that the territory of the neutral Pontifical State was respected.

The American diarist observed these Nazi paratroopers carrying tommy guns in St. Peter's Square and adds a further detail that the dry, almost clinical, newspaper story did not: "The Vatican officials referred to were the commanders of the Swiss Guard and the Palatine Guard."[12] In late 1943, the Swiss commandant was Heinrich Pfyffer von Altishofen, the first member of that distinguished family to hold the post in almost a century.

In a way, this development was not surprising: who else would have undertaken these negotiations about patrolling the perimeter of the Vatican City State and its relations with the occupiers of Rome? But perhaps the more difficult and complicated task facing the Swiss was keeping the Romans themselves calm. Much controversy has arisen in recent years over whether Pius XII should have spoken out more forcefully about the rounding up and wholesale slaughter of the Jews by the Nazi regime. A whole library of books making charges and countering those charges now exists. Whatever might be said on that score, the pope had to walk a very fine line in Rome to make sure that the Italian Christians themselves, as well as Italian Jews and others, did not suffer a bloodbath. In Naples, spontaneous acts of resistance to the Germans had led to many deaths, and the Romans wanted to avoid pointless sacrifices that might even be counterproductive for the common goal — freeing the city from Nazi occupation. Our diarist repeatedly observes that the random acts of violence against the Germans in the city merely led to reprisals against innocent people. The only prudent thing for the Romans to do at the time was to remain calm and wait for the Allied forces to draw closer or the Germans to withdraw numbers of troops and therefore make the struggle less futile.

The specific way in which the Swiss guards assisted in keeping calm was to prevent a rush into the Vatican on the part of people seeking a kind of asylum. If such a surge had happened, our diarist assures us, the Swiss "would never fire on a crowd of that kind." But if a large number of people were to make their way into the Vatican, it would have immensely complicated the negotiations with the Germans and many other tasks that the Holy See was carrying out at the time. As it was, many people huddled under the colonnades of St. Peter's during the Allied air strikes on the city, rightly believing that American and British planes would not deliberately attack the Vatican. According to reliable studies, in addition to its other services to the city, the Holy See was feeding at least fifteen thousand people a day around this period. Trucks marked on the roof *Vaticano* (Vatican State) to warn both Allied and German planes that they were not part of either side's war effort brought in huge amounts of food for both the Holy See and the many in Rome it sought to support. For the most part, these trucks moved unmolested around the country, but they could not keep up with the rapidly growing need in Nazi-occupied Rome.

A Swiss Guard's Firsthand Account

Not many firsthand documents by the Swiss guards have survived from the period, perhaps partly owing to the fact that things written down at such a time ran the risk of finding their way into unfriendly hands — and producing unwelcome consequences. But a later memoir by Alexander Good, a young halberdier in Rome precisely during the most danger-laden days (1943–46), gives a vivid account of day-to-day life under the German occupation.[13] Good was on duty at the Bronze Doors the night that the bombs fell behind St. Peter's Basilica. Moments before the explosion, he and the other guards were engaged in casual joking. When the series of loud explosions began, it sent shards of glass flying from the windows, rattled the halberds in their stands, and knocked the rifles and their bayonets out of their wooden racks onto the marble floor. Nothing like this had ever happened before at the Vatican, and between the sheer force of the explosions and the utter surprise, the young guards were momentarily stunned. They were soon called back to their senses: "We were still shocked by the event when the telephone at the post rang. The 'Maestro di casa' [house master] was calling the Swiss Guard Central Post to find out what had happened." In the first moments, everyone assumed that St. Peter's Basilica had been hit.

The Swiss went out and discovered that four bombs had fallen: one near the western reservoir, another directly behind the building where the Vatican's Governatorato, or civil government, is housed, a third a direct hit on the mosaic workshop, and the fourth near the Vatican train station, rupturing a water main that was now spurting water several meters into the air. The Governatorato palace and the mosaic shop had sustained the worst damage. Fortunately, no one had been killed, though one of the papal gendarmes on duty at the Governatorato had been knocked down by the blast and showered with glass. He was shaken, but only lightly wounded. Whoever had carried out the attack and whatever their intentions, St. Peter's remained mostly unharmed; there was some damage to its windows, particularly the yellow stained-glass depiction of the Holy Spirit as a descending dove at the very back of the church. The damage to the Vatican City overall was frightening, but under the circumstances it could have been very much worse.

Halberdier Good reports one unintended benefit to the guards from the air raid, *Glück im Unglück* (Fortune in misfortune), as he calls it. The scout they sent out entered the Governatorato Palace to assess the bomb damage. The cellar had been particularly hard hit and was in total chaos. About a hundred bottles of the finest cognac had been knocked to the floor and broken into pieces. A pool of the liquor six inches high had formed. Rather than let it go totally to waste, the scout went back to get his comrades to help deal with the problem: "Yes indeed, the pope's Swiss guards know how to make themselves useful in such situations," commented Halberdier Good. It was the guards' consolation for the fact that, from that point on, no one could any longer rely on the Vatican as a safe haven from outside attack. Until the end of the war, they had to assume that anything was possible at any time and try, as best they might, to be prepared for any kind of violent assault.

The bombs fell in the Vatican in November 1943. Christmas that year was naturally quite bleak. The mails to Switzerland had been blocked by the Germans, and long-distance telephone service was, at best, intermittent and mostly too expensive for the average young guard. The usual homesickness, a disease first diagnosed by doctors observing the Swiss guards in Rome, was exacerbated by the feeling of complete isolation. At this point in the occupation of Rome, the guards were fortunate that they still had provisions that enabled them to hold a traditional Christmas celebration complete with pastries, tangerines, nuts, and other goodies. But they ate their dinner and drank their toasts in silence that year; even the Christmas tree and carols did not much lift their spirits: "'Silent Night — Holy Night,' was sung, but not very convincingly," reported Good.

By January 1944, the general shortages of food, fuel, and supplies that were affecting the citizens of Rome began to be felt sharply inside the Vatican as well. The Holy See's trucks continued to bring food into the city, but the advance of the Allies from the south brought even more refugees to Rome who needed to be fed and housed. Butter, cheese, salami, and jam disappeared from the canteen in the Swiss guards' barracks. Some unidentifiable sweet brown substance took the place of the jam, and an equally dubious material was substituted for coffee — an important eye-opener for young men who have to keep long watches. Even bread started to be rationed, and the rations themselves were periodically reduced. In the Swiss Army at home, each soldier was allowed 500 grams (a little over one pound) of bread per day at the time. Among the Swiss guards in Rome, the ration was set at half that and was soon reduced even further to only 150 grams per day.

The guards sometimes felt they could not, in good conscience, eat even that much. Some of the children of the families who had been forced to flee to Rome would show up at the grated windows between the kitchen and the mess hall that opened through the walls of the Vatican onto the Roman streets of the Borgo Pio. They were impossible to ignore, and the guards would pass bits of bread to them. Halberdier Good recalls that the PAI (Polizia Africana Italiana), an African corps of the Italian Army, would often show up without notice and drive the children away from the Vatican walls: "We loathed these booted accomplices of the Fascist Dictatorship and their pitiless intervention at the border of the sovereign Vatican City State." Good could not know much about it, but bread riots were beginning to break out in the city of Rome around April 1944 and would continue until the city was liberated by the Allies. One of the few things the guards still had in abundance, however, even as they were forced to a kind of "Lenten Fast," says Good, was the light white wine of the Castelli Romani, long a special favorite of the guards and generously provided over the centuries by the Holy See: "It took the place of the essential caloric requirements — and we hardly considered that a penance."

Kidnapping the Pope?

A particular danger that the guards were acutely aware of, since it had been discussed for years inside the Vatican, was a Nazi attempt to kidnap the pope and take him to Germany. In the summer of 1943, the pope had already summoned all the cardinals living in Rome to discuss that possibility. As one historian describes the further measures:

> Documents were stashed in unlikely places, and Pius [XII]'s personal files were buried under the marble floors of the papal palace. Adding to the drama was the smoke wafting in the great interiors as Allied diplomats residing in the Vatican put the files to flame. The dreaded moment seemed at hand, and according to a Vatican document, the commandant of the Swiss Guards was told that it was the Pope's wish that his men offer no resistance to a German takeover of Vatican City.[14]

In fact, Hitler had worked out such a plan and had asked SS General Karl Wolff to implement it. Wolff later claimed that he agreed in the face-to-face meeting with the Führer to abduct the pope, but by that point (September 12, 1943) he believed that Nazi policy was doomed and only pretended to be planning the abduction.[15] He was also supposed to loot large amounts of Vatican art along with books and manuscripts from the Vatican Library. Wolff may have been telling the truth. Other German officials such as the ambassador to the Holy See, Baron Ernst von Weizsäcker, also learned of the idea and thought it mad, since it would give the Allies even greater incentive to invade Rome.

The Final Assault and the Liberation of Rome

As the Vatican forces nervously tried to plan what to do in case of a German attack and kidnapping of the pope, the Allied forces in Italy began to advance more rapidly and, none too soon for almost everyone in Rome, to drive out the German occupation forces. The month of March in 1944 revealed how explosive a situation the Vatican and the guards faced. On March 12, Pius XII celebrated the fifth anniversary of his election as pope. Fascist laws had no jurisdiction over the Vatican, so their ban on public assemblies could be safely ignored. Reliable observers estimated that a hundred thousand people crowded into St. Peter's Square to hear the pope's remarks on behalf of peace, which included a denunciation of Allied air raids that risked destroying Rome, as they had other European cities. Groups belonging to the Committees for National Liberation (CLN), an umbrella resistance organization, had secretly prepared a demonstration, and as soon as the pope finished speaking, people positioned within the enormous crowd began to call for the departure of the Germans from Rome, since they were the real target of the Allied bombings. The Vatican seems to have had some advanced warning about the demonstrations because it had set up some barriers near the basilica and stationed Swiss guards behind them to keep the crowd under control.[16]

As has already been noted above, Pius XII has been both praised for saving the city of Rome and condemned for failing to speak out more forcefully against the crimes against Jews and other Romans.[17] Whatever might be concluded about his actions, an outbreak of resistance shortly after this anniversary event showed what ill-advised violence could produce. On March 23, the twenty-fifth anniversary of the birth of the Italian Fascist Party, some elements within the CLN planted a bomb on the Via Rasella, near the Palazzo Barberini in the center of Rome, and set it off as 156 SS troops were marching by. Thirty-two Germans died immediately and many more suffered wounds. When Hitler heard of the attack, he ordered ten Italians to be killed for every German who had died. The German and Fascist forces selected more than 330 political prisoners and others, transported them to the Ardeatine Caves in the southern part of Rome, and executed them all, sealing up the natural grave. All this immediately became known and produced both shock and caution on the part of all those responsible for the welfare of the city. Fortunately, things changed before such outrages could be repeated.

In fact, Halberdier Alexander Good tells of a curious coincidence: May 6, 1944, was a typically bright spring day in Rome, and he and a group of comrades were to be sworn formally into papal service at a ceremony in the Cortile of the Belvedere (alongside the Vatican Museums and the Cortile San Damaso, where the ceremony has usually been held in more recent years). Like all modern Swiss guards, though he had been part of the corps since being recruited the previous year, he had had to wait until May 6, the day each year when everyone commemorates the guards who fell during the sack of Rome, in order to swear his loyalty to the pope. As he and his brothers came forward to take hold of the flag and recite the oath, something unprecedented occurred:

> Man after man marched in single file to the flag, meanwhile there passed over our heads a squadron of bombers taking a course towards the center of the city of Rome on a bombing run. Exactly at the moment that our comrade Maurizio Ebener raised his hand to swear in front of the Guard banner, there followed several detonations, whose shocks we perceived clearly there in the Cortile of the Belvedere. The booming that occurred made clear and unmistakable to us the seriousness of the moment and our heavy responsibility, the responsibility we were assuming with our swearing the oath on the flag. Who knew what might await us in the near future?

Those bombers were Allied planes, British and American, and happily, for Good and everyone else in Rome, in less than a month (June 5) General Mark Clark and the British and American armies liberated Rome to great jubilation and with relatively light damage to the city — and almost none to the Vatican itself. A few days later, flanked by Swiss guards, Pope Pius XII offered prayers of thanksgiving for the happy outcome from the *loggia* of St. Peter's.

Chapter Eight

Modern Times

THE POSTWAR PERIOD, especially the 1950s, was one of relief and relative calm for Italy, the Vatican, and the guards, though some problems emerged even then. In 1951, the guards were agitated again, this time over money matters. They were receiving the equivalent of only about $50 a month, and prices had risen painfully in Italy after the war. Raises and restructuring of the Guard did not come until the late 1950s, however. In the meantime, Heinrich Pfyffer von Altishofen died in 1957 after fifteen years as commandant, the first two in the precarious war years. It was only at his death that it was revealed that he had asked Pope Pius XII for permission to fire if the Germans attacked, but had been refused. His successor, Robert Nünlist, was a colonel in the Swiss Army and former professor of philosophy. Nünlist himself spent fifteen years (1957–72) as commandant, during which several disturbing incidents occurred. Two years after he had been named head of the Swiss Guard, he was shot and slightly wounded by Adolfo Rueckers, one of his own assistants, in the courtyard of the Swiss barracks. Rueckers had been dismissed from service because he had become an epileptic after a head injury. Nünlist disarmed him and soon recovered from his wounds.

In the 1960s, modern terrorist threats began to touch the Vatican, which Nünlist and his men had to take increasingly into account and had to prepare themselves to thwart. The Second Vatican Council (1962–65) brought to Rome over two thousand bishops from around the world. In addition to them, thousands of theological advisers, aides, and journalists had to be kept in order during the council sessions, which were held in St. Peter's Basilica. In the year the council opened, a bomb exploded in St. Peter's; fortunately no one was harmed, and it did little damage to the church. Just before one of the council sessions that same year, security forces discovered two more bombs that had been placed in the basilica; these were defused without incident. In 1965, a bomb exploded near the Sant'Anna Gate, the principal entrance to the Vatican City State, which the guards control. Fortunately, no one was injured, but the blast blew out the windows in the guards' quarters. No one ever took responsibility for any of these bombings, but the best sources believe these incidents were the beginnings of the much greater wave of bombings and kidnappings by left-wing Italian groups such as the Red Brigades that gripped Italy in the 1970s.

As we saw in the first chapter, it was in September of 1970 that Pope Paul VI decided to abolish all the existing Vatican security forces except the Swiss Guard and to set up alternative arrangements more in keeping with the modern papacy. As he said at the time, he took these steps "to insure that everything that surrounds the successor of Peter should clearly manifest the religious nature of his mission, which is ever more sincerely inspired by unreserved evangelical simplicity." The modern papacy, separated from direct political power as it had not been since the later Middle Ages and perhaps even as far back as the end of the Roman Empire, certainly needed to reflect its contemporary nature in every detail, but part of that nature and many of the details did not allow for quite as great a nonchalance about security as Pope Paul's generous character and good intentions might have mistakenly implied. An attempt on his own life during a visit to the Philippines in December of 1970 — just a few months after he announced the reorganization — already showed that the modern papacy, however evangelical and simple, faced real threats as it went out into the wide world.

Paul VI went on a pilgrimage through several Asian countries toward the end of 1970. It was a bold new departure for the papacy, because instead of visiting the usual European nations, the pope had chosen much more challenging destinations such as Iran, Pakistan, Indonesia, and Hong Kong, along with several other small states. The only "Western" country he visited was Australia and the only predominantly Catholic one, the Philippines. Ironically, it was in the Philippine capital, Manila, that a deranged Bolivian painter, Benjamin Mendoza, was able to step out in front of the pope even before he had gotten to the airport podium to pronounce his first words. The attacker had a long knife in one hand and a crucifix in the other and was quickly subdued by security forces. How he had been able to penetrate security in a country where the president, Ferdinand Marcos (who was present), was frequently threatened was never fully explained. But the event was a harbinger of many such threats to come.

Franz Pfyffer von Altishofen, a lawyer from Lucerne, succeeded Robert Nünlist as commander of the guards in 1972. For the next decade, this latest representative of the family that had provided so many volunteers and leaders for the papal service (eleven commandants and thirty men overall) had to confront the modern threats to the pope, including the attempt on John Paul II in St. Peter's Square on May 13, 1981. That failed assassination shocked the world and brought home to many people that even the pope was not beyond the reach of would-be modern murderers. But it was not entirely unanticipated by the Swiss guards and others charged with protecting the pope. In fact, papal security services had been reorganized in several ways in the decade or so before Mehmet Ali Agca, a Turk previously convicted of murdering a journalist in Turkey, stepped out of the crowd and fired two shots that struck the pontiff. Agca was a member of the Turkish terrorist group the Grey Wolves, and it seems all but certain, though it has never been fully proven, that he was assisted by Bulgarian Communist special services acting ultimately under the direction of the Soviet KGB. As everyone connected with protecting the pope was aware, however, it would not take a very sophisticated effort to attack a pope like John Paul II, who insisted on being in as close contact as possible with the people, whatever the risks to his own personal safety.

All modern public figures, however, face such risks. Just two months earlier, a mentally unstable young man had succeeded in a similar attempt on President Reagan as he was exiting a Washington hotel and about to step into the presidential limousine just a few feet away, despite the protection of the U.S. Secret Service. Whatever help Agca had received from sophisticated intelligence agencies, his attempt made plain how the nature of the papacy in particular exposes popes to would-be attackers. In the case of John Paul II, an even worse result was avoided because the Swiss guards and other security forces on duty that day had a clear and well-coordinated plan to get the wounded pontiff to an ambulance and then off to the Gemelli Polyclinic. Given Roman traffic jams, the pope could easily have bled to death without such prior arrangements, which included quickly informing the Rome traffic police to open up and keep open the route to the hospital.

Roland Buchs-Bins, a native of Fribourg, served as commandant from 1982 to 1998, which is to say for seventeen of the twenty-six years of John Paul II's papacy, and the most active and exposed years at that. He also has the unique distinction of being the only person in history to have served twice as commandant: first, during his regular tour of duty, and then again in 1998 as a temporary substitute after the commandant was tragically killed by one of his own guards the very day that the new leader had been selected by the Holy See. Buchs had come to the guards as a major in 1976 at the request of his local bishop and the papal nuncio to Switzerland. He had never served in the Guard previously, which is not at all uncommon since about half of the higher officers have been recruited from outside the Guard. In 1976, the papacy of Paul VI was winding down, and the recruiters sought in Buchs someone who would be able to help the commandant with administrative and financial matters. Since Buchs had commanded a battalion in the Swiss Army and had worked with Swiss banking firms, in addition to being a prominent Catholic, he seemed the ideal person for the post. The original plan was for him to remain for ten years in Rome, but in 1982, when Franz Pfyffer von Altishofen retired, Buchs's good work as an officer made him the logical choice to succeed.

The tasks he had to carry out were quite a bit different from the administrative and financial affairs he had been recruited to manage. As second-in-command, he had also been in charge of the training of new recruits. After the attempts on the pope's life, that training had to include new methods of protecting the person of the pope in crowds. Senior commanders of Swiss police and security forces were invited to come to Rome each year and spend a week training the men in the latest security techniques. The highest-ranking general in the Swiss Army officially visited the Vatican for the first time in history and consigned up-to-date pistols, automatic rifles, and other standard Swiss Army weapons to the Papal Swiss Guard for as long as the corps remains in papal service. A rethinking of every aspect of the guarding of the Holy Father, begun under Pfyffer von Altishofen, continued. In the Apostolic Palace, a system of security checks was put in place that includes identification badges and visiting permits, and even technologically advanced electronic cards for access to certain areas. The papal residence at present enjoys quite strict but unobtrusive security. Anyone who visits the Holy Father must pass multiple Swiss checkpoints.

The style of John Paul's papacy, however, as Buchs has admitted, made 100 percent security impossible, since, if the pope wishes to walk over and greet a crowd, the Swiss guards are not about to deny him access — even if they know there are many risks. The most they can do is to offer as flexible a service as possible in the circumstances. John Paul and his successor, Benedict XVI, have publicly and frequently praised the guards for making their efforts to reach out to people a more secure undertaking, but both of them have also often enough simply ignored the advice of their security agents when they think the papal mission requires it. On most occasions, numerous plain-clothes guards and other Vatican security forces are mixed in with the crowds at papal events. At least since the 1981 shooting of John Paul, there are also guards observing the crowds with binoculars from positions above St. Peter's Square. In the aftermath of that event, the guards re-evaluated the best methods of keeping escape routes open as well. Plans in place in 1981 had made it possible to get the pope to a hospital quickly and thereby prevent him from bleeding to death. But more severe wounds might have called for even faster action. The Swiss guards have done virtually everything humanly possible to secure the person of the pope in a way in keeping with his role as head of the Catholic Church and the Vatican City State, but also as a universal pastor.

Contemporary Threats

The modern demands on the Swiss Guard and other Vatican security forces protecting the pope are probably greater than for any other public figure, including the president of the United States. An American president usually remains at a reasonably safe distance from threats of violence, though in a 2005 visit to the former Soviet republic of Georgia a live hand grenade landed only a hundred feet from President George W. Bush. Political leaders generally accept the fact that their political offices require security measures that separate them from the public. Modern popes have chosen to do the exact opposite, believing that the Vicar of Christ has to be in close contact with the faithful. Paul VI did not possess the outgoing personality of his predecessor Pope John XXIII, nor was he a globe-trotter like his successor John Paul II, but even Paul felt the duty of making contact with people in ways that no security service would tolerate for a political leader. John Paul II was notorious throughout the years of his papacy for ignoring the advice of his security people. He even refused to take such simple precautions as not accepting flowers or other presents in crowds, things that might contain explosives or poisons. He often said that his bodyguard was "divine providence." His successor, Benedict XVI, immediately began to speak and act in similar ways following his election as pope in May 2005.

There have been many more earthly "guardian angels" who have helped out divine providence in recent decades, the Swiss guards prominently among them. Two officers of the guards in plain clothes, usually the commandant and one of his lieutenants, accompany the pope virtually everywhere he travels outside of the Vatican. A knowledgeable commentator has written of them: "The Swiss are ultra-close-range 'guardian angels,' and serve in cases of attacks at point-blank-range, kidnaps, and the possible need to form a 'human shield.'" He contrasts them with the other forces: "The Corpo di Vigilanza, instead, besides furnishing police escorts that are always present alongside the Holy Father in his comings and goings, 'interface' with the Italian Inspectorate of Public Safety assigned to the Vatican."[1] As a general description, this is not wholly wrong, though all three bodies collaborate quite closely in the protection of the pope when he travels in Italy (when he travels abroad, the Swiss Guard and the Corpo di Vigilanza work with local and national security agencies such as the U.S. FBI and Secret Service).

When the three main bodyguard services want to exert the fullest possible control over the pope's safety, the result is as impressive as that for any world figure. Italian secret service agents in tailored suits (with concealed automatic weapons) establish an outer perimeter, while the Corpo di Vigilanza and the Swiss Guard form concentric rings within that area. In the nature of things, however, much depends on what the pope himself wishes to happen. It is common in Rome, for example, to see crowds pressing in quite close to papal vehicles when the pontiff decides, as bishop of the city, to appear at some church or celebrate some religious occasion. The Italian inspector of public safety Gerardo Centanni has remarked, "I protect him primarily from enthusiasm," and that is exactly what can be seen almost every day as crowds move in to get a close look at the pope as he passes through the streets of Rome. But the worried faces of the men closer in, especially the Swiss, reflect a constant concern that the pope's nearness to the people, however much necessary, presents a threat that even the most watchful escort cannot entirely guard against.

There has been ample reason for worry over the past thirty-five years. Since the 1970 attempt on Paul VI in Manila, dozens of threats to the pope have surfaced. Popes have, of course, been in mortal danger since the time of St. Peter, but the apparent peacefulness that followed the Second World War led many people into a false sense of security. As the Cold War emerged, many new actors developed an interest in who is pope and what goes on in the Vatican. One of the questions that had to be decided in Italy after the defeat of Nazism and Fascism, for example, was whether the nation would return to the monarchy of the house of Savoy that had existed since 1870 or would establish a new democratic republic. It would have surprised nineteenth-century popes such as Gregory XVI and Pius IX, but their successors Pius XII — the wartime pope — and Giovanni Battista Montini (later Paul VI) favored the monarchy. When the Italians decided otherwise, the Vatican had to deal with the growing influence of the Communist Party in Italy, which could lead to no good for Catholicism. Although opinions vary about how closely the Vatican cooperated with the American OSS and other Western intelligence agencies, that there was cooperation is beyond all doubt. And Archbishop Montini, prior to becoming pope, seems to have had a central role in intelligence matters.

All this was a mere prelude, however, by comparison with the political prominence of the Vatican after the election of the Polish cardinal Karol Wojtyla as Pope John Paul II in October 1978. When electronic bugs were later discovered in the Vatican, notably in a small statue in the dining room of Cardinal Agostino Casaroli, John Paul's close associate and Vatican secretary of state, it was no surprise to anyone. That and other listening devices had been planted by the Soviets, and Wojtyla already had ample experience back home in Poland in dealing with such Communist contrivances. He is said to have joked that he was going to recite the rosary into the microphones and convert the eavesdroppers. It was more surprising, however, when it was revealed in the 1990s that the Italian intelligence service SISMI (Servizi Informazioni Segreto Militare Italiano) had also bugged the pope's apartments, primarily, it seems, to keep informed about his developing stance toward the Warsaw Pact nations. And it is a safe bet that other nations besides the Soviet Union and Italy took steps to keep close tabs on the Polish pontiff. Evidence exists that the conclave that elected him was also under secret surveillance.

Though these measures were a problem and may have been used to plan more direct threats on Wojtyla, other dangers were also close at hand. In December 1979, a little over a year after the pope was elected, Francesco Pasanisi became head of the Italian security services protecting the pope. Pasanisi had already served as head of the security escort for the Italian president and was clearly brought in to organize things in ways that the Swiss, Vatican security, and even the usual Italian secret service were not up to. Just before his move to the position protecting the pope, John Paul II had decided to reach out to Orthodox believers in the eastern Mediterranean and to the Islamic world by visiting Turkey. In a harbinger of things to come, the visit was not welcome by all Turks and was viewed with no little suspicion by Muslims in general. A then unknown Turk, Mehmet Ali Agca, who had escaped from a Turkish prison, circulated a threat that he would kill the pope if he came to Turkey. Fortunately, nothing happened during the visit — perhaps because the Turks mobilized ten thousand security agents.

A series of more worrisome events followed, however. John Paul II began his trademark globe-trotting in 1980. In early 1981, he went to Karachi, Pakistan. There a bomb went off close to an altar where he was to say Mass, only twenty minutes before he arrived. Agca shot the pope in St. Peter's Square two months later. The pope publicly forgave Agca and, after recovering, did not change his intentions to visit Catholics and non-Catholics all over the world. But from that point on it seems that the CIA, the British agency MI-6, and other Western intelligence services began feeding the Vatican information on security threats before the pope was to travel. Even these sophisticated sources, however, have a limited utility, and the only really effective remedy is the old-fashioned bodyguard. When John Paul II went to the shrine at Fatima in Portugal one year after the shooting in thanksgiving that, as he believed, the Blessed Virgin Mary had intervened to save him from the assassin, another would-be murderer — this time a fanatical priest, Juan Fernandez Krohn, who belonged to a traditionalist movement that contends Vatican II taught heresy and the pope in Rome was a usurper — leapt out of the crowd with a knife over a foot long. He had to be subdued by the security detail, which consisted of two Swiss guards and two members of the Vatican Corpo di Vigilanza.

Attempts on the pope's life followed him, year by year, wherever he went:

- In Toronto, Canada, in 1984, a man with a knife (who had stolen his invitation to a gathering with the pope) was arrested by police just prior to the pope's arrival.

- In Lima, Peru, in 1985, the Marxist guerilla group Sendero Luminoso indirectly threatened the pope by declaring the area he was visiting a "war zone"; John Paul was able to visit a slum area only because of a massive police presence; three years later when he came to Peru again, the threats repeated themselves.

- In Holland in 1985, Aslan Samet, a Turk, was arrested in possession of a Browning 9mm pistol a few day before John Paul's visit; further investigation showed he was a member of the Turkish terrorist organization the Gray Wolves and that he had ties to Mehmet Ali Agca; later, it became clear that Samet was actually Oral Celik, Agca's accomplice in the attack on the pope.

- In Brisbane, Australia, in 1986 an Irish man, Richard John McLaughlin, was stopped by police after suspicious behavior and found to have five Molotov cocktails in a box; he was looking for the best place to launch them against the visiting pope; a thousand plain-clothes police were in the crowd at the Mass to keep an eye on other possible threats.

- In 1994, John Paul tried to visit Lebanon, but because bombs went off in several churches there and a bomb was found in a stadium where he was to say Mass, he put off the trip, not because of fear for himself but because of the potential loss of life among Lebanese Christians and others.

- In the Philippines in 1995, local police happened upon a Muslim terrorist cell preparing bombs to use against the pope; they had disguises so that they could pass for priests; the CIA and Philippine intelligence discovered evidence than an Iraqi agent was shadowing the pontiff on his trip; four members of the Corpo di Vigilanza and two Swiss guards formed a special escort squad after news that a plastic gun, invisible to metal detectors, might have been smuggled into the country; Ramzi Ahmed Yousef, who had planned the first attack on the World Trade Center in 1993, was involved.

- In Nicaragua in 1996 some of the same Sandinista elements who had organized a massive demonstration during the pope's Mass in Managua in the 1980s went into action again; the pope had to wait for an armored "popemobile" to be flown in before he could visit.

- In Sarajevo, Bosnia, in 1997 the pope wanted to drive down "snipers' alley" from the airport so that average people would be able to see him upon arrival; security forces found twenty-three mines along the route; the Swiss and others in the papal security team were forced for the first time ever to wear bulletproof vests during the Mass; Turkish and Iranian terror networks were later linked to the situation; evidence surfaced

of intentions to detonate a bomb along the papal route in St. Peter's Square as well.
- In India in 1999, Muslim groups linked to Osama bin Laden planned an attack on the pope to discredit the Indian government; massive security measures, including bomb-sniffing dogs, prevented any serious threat from reaching the pope.
- In Israel in 2000, John Paul II's pilgrimage had far-reaching effects on Catholic-Jewish relations, but nearly twenty-five thousand Israeli police and soldiers were deployed for security in what the Israeli government called Operation Old Friend.
- In Syria in 2001, the American CIA foiled a suicide bombing against the pope by a woman who was part of a terrorist cell that planned the effort and was prepared to kill all survivors.
- On a visit to Kazhakstan just ten days after the 2001 suicide attacks on the World Trade Center towers in New York and the Pentagon in Washington, the papal plane was for the first time escorted along the whole route by fighter jets from the countries John Paul was flying over.
- In Croatia in 2003, death threats surfaced against the visiting pope and "the infidels" by a Muslim group; by then, the papal entourage was so used to threats that they had become a routine part of the pope's visits.

Somehow the security forces during this entire period managed to succeed in the balancing act between allowing the crowds to be close to the pope but not too close, or at least not dangerously so. It was a minor miracle that their record was so good.

An Unfortunate Interlude

When Roland Buchs retired in 1998, the Holy See was slow to find a replacement for him. Five months passed before the Vatican selected Alois Estermann, one of the papal bodyguards who had been walking alongside the popemobile when John Paul was shot in St. Peter's Square in 1981. One of the most shocking events in the entire history of the Swiss Guard came completely without warning on May 4, 1998. Around nine o'clock in the evening after a long day of drilling by the new recruits who were to be sworn in two days later, loud shouts and noises were briefly heard in the Estermann apartment. He had just been named as the new commandant of the Guard earlier that very day. Sister Anna-Lina Meier, a member of the Sisters of Divine Providence of Baldegg, Switzerland, who performed various tasks in the Swiss barracks, went out to see what the noise was all about. She found the door to the Estermann apartment open and could see the body of the colonel's wife on the floor inside. Afraid to go any further on her own, she looked for someone in authority and came upon Lance Corporal Marcel Riedi. Riedi entered the apartment cautiously in case an intruder might still be present. What he found was horrifying. Not only had the colonel and his wife been shot, but another lance corporal, Cédric Tornay, also lay dead with his service SIG 9mm pistol underneath him, an apparent suicide.

As might be expected, the scene gave rise to multiple speculations. Gladys Meza Romero, Estermann's wife, had been a model in her native Venezuela before quitting to become a policewoman. When she moved to Rome and married Estermann, she worked at the Venezuelan Embassy, and the two of them were a glamorous couple in diplomatic circles. One early rumor had it that she and Tornay had had an affair that went bad, leading to the dual murder and suicide. But this rather typical sordid formula did not satisfy some scandalmongers. Soon other rumors were circulating that Estermann had been a homosexual and the relationship that had soured was between him and young Tornay. In this scenario, Meza Romero had been killed merely by chance as the drama was being played out. Even that story, however, was not the end of speculations. Since Estermann had been among the guards walking alongside the popemobile in St. Peter's Square when John Paul II was shot by Mehmet Ali Agca in 1981, and Agca seems to have had assistance from the Communists, a third theory appeared in the press: Estermann had secretly been an agent (code name "Werder") for the East German secret police, the Stasi. But some writers then insisted that, on the contrary, he was involved in some sinister way with Opus Dei. Depending on the source, it has been claimed that Tornay found out about the Stasi or Opus Dei connections, and felt honor-bound to prevent Estermann from assuming his new duties as commandant of the Swiss Guard for the good of the Catholic Church.

Though all these stories held sway in tabloid and other publications for some time after the unfortunate event, the reality seems to have been much simpler and far less lurid. Several investigative reporters have written books on the case trying to substantiate the wilder claims, including the Rome correspondent of the London *Sunday Times*.[2] In spite of visits to former Stasi officers, probes into homosexual circles in Rome, and interviews with dozens of people in London, Paris, Italy, and Switzerland, no credible evidence of any of the scenarios mentioned above has emerged. Instead, it appears that Tornay simply snapped that day. Roland Buchs, who had preceded Estermann as commandant, knew Tornay personally, and at the funeral in Tornay's home town of Saint-Maurice described Tornay as "sensitive to the way other people treated him, and their reactions affected him deeply.... His act remains mysterious. Who can understand his last gesture? At this tragic time, many 'whys' and 'wherefores' remain in suspense. Only God knows the answers to our questions."[3]

Tornay clearly had accumulated grievances — he calls them "injustices" in a suicide note to his family, which itself argues against the wilder theories. At least in his own view, these stemmed from the personal harshness and unfairness of Colonel Estermann toward him, and even some smoldering tension between the German- and French-speaking members of the Guard, a division that exists in Switzerland itself as well. Whether these complaints were real or imagined, or some mixture of the two, is impossible now to establish. What is indisputable is that the immediate cause of his rage and the spark that set him off seems to have been that, because of previous disciplinary infractions, Estermann abruptly denied him a *benemerenti* medal, an almost automatic reward to guards after three years' service. Tornay seems to have decided to hold out long enough in the guards at least to get that sign of recognition. Being abruptly denied his chance just two days before it would have occurred was the last straw. His family has disputed this explanation but has not offered any better one. And his mother may have made a serious error for their case in hiring Jacques Vergès as the family lawyer. Vergès is a well-known, high-profile litigator in Europe who in the past has defended the international terrorist Carlos the Jackal, the Nazi leader Klaus Barbie, and Serbian president Slobodan Milošević. The unsavory associations with these notorious cases may have the unfortunate effect of obscuring whatever real merit Tornay's claims of "injustices" may have had.

Perhaps the most fitting commentary on these sad facts was spoken by John Paul II who, at the funeral, said that Tornay was in front of the judgment seat of God "to whose mercy I entrust him." Of the guards in general, Cardinal Sodano, Vatican secretary of state, said, "Dear officers of the Holy See, the pope renews his trust and his gratitude. The black cloud of one day cannot obscure more than five hundred years of service."[4] Roland Buchs came out of retirement temporarily as the Holy See looked for replacements.

New Directions

Perhaps as a way to remove the guards from their immersion in the recent tragedy, the pope named two officers who had never done previous service in the Swiss Guard. Pius Segmüller, the new commandant, was a man of many talents. He had reached the rank of colonel in the Swiss Army, done relief work in Africa and police service in Switzerland, and also taught history and literature. His new second-in-command officer, Elmar Theodor Mäder, was also a Swiss Army officer, in addition to being a lawyer who had run a financial services company. The well-spoken Mäder was named commandant at Segmüller's retirement in 2002 and commanded the guards as they celebrated their five hundredth anniversary in 2006.

Segmüller and Mäder had to meet a new challenge. The Jubilee celebration of 2000 attracted even more massive crowds than usual to Rome and involved many special Vatican events, owing to John Paul II's decision to spend the three years prior to the date in promoting the notion of the Third Christian Millennium. All of this activity had incalculable benefits for both the Catholic Church and the city of Rome itself. But for the Swiss Guard, whose numbers have pretty much remained the same from year to year, it meant pushing the number of man-hours in service to the breaking point. They reached an all-time high of service hours in 2000; fortunately, their responsibilities have since sunk back toward more normal levels. During the worst times, however, they had to resort to an innovative solution: ex-guards who were old enough to retire in Switzerland came back to Rome for periods of a few months. They were not asked to do any of the heavy guard duty. Instead, they did the jobs in the canteen and the guards' headquarters that otherwise can take up the time of three or four men — not a problem during normal periods but a significant help during the Jubilee Year.

Special events may be a burden for guards in service, but they are a wonderful tool for recruiting. In the months immediately following the death of John Paul II and the election of his successor, Benedict XVI, for example, about one hundred young Swiss presented themselves as candidates for the Swiss Guard. Not all of them were suitable, and there is some natural attrition as minds change during the application process. But it is no small matter when a papal succession stimulates almost as many applicants as there are guards in active service. Numbers on that scale could make life easier for all the guards. Special events are important, but perhaps the large crop of applications indicates that there is a large pool of potential guards if they were to be approached with the kinds of means that are most effective in an age of omnipresent electronic media. Authoritative voices in Switzerland such as that of bishop of Chur Amédée Grab believe that all Swiss, Protestants as well as Catholics, are proud of the unusual little force that their confederation has supplied. Drawing on that pride might solve any manpower questions.

There was a similar bumper crop of would-be recruits in the mid-1980s following the election of a non-Italian pope for the first time in five hundred years, the unsuccessful attempt on his life in 1981, and the growing importance of John Paul II on the world stage. What was even more surprising, according to Roland Buchs, who was commandant of the Guard at the time, a number of Protestant families tried to get their sons into the Swiss Guard.[5] As in most places in the world today, Catholics and Protestants are not as much at odds with one another in Switzerland as they were in the past. All Swiss take pride in the unique role Swiss military men play in the Vatican. And among the reasons often mentioned by the Protestants seeking admission to the Swiss Guard were the continuation of a tradition, a rich history, and a certain idealism. The pope as Christian leader did not present an obstacle at all, apparently, in light of a wish to connect with something good in Switzerland's own past.

Along with the development of the papacy from Leo XIII to John Paul II, the sequence of Swiss commandants in the twentieth century and beyond, from Leopold Meyer von Schauensee to Elmar Mäder, shows an interesting evolution and the changing nature of the guards. Meyer was the son of a commandant and part of the older-style military tradition of the guards. It was an honorable tradition stretching back to Julius II and Kaspar Röist, but to be faithful to what the tradition aimed at, the safety of the pope, that tradition has had to develop during the twentieth century in directions that popes from Pius X to John XXIII, and from Paul VI to John Paul II himself realized were demanded of the Swiss corps by the nature of the contemporary world. Under

Elmar Mäder, the Swiss guards have had to draw closer to the spiritual mission, even as they have had to learn more sophisticated and serious security techniques. As John Paul II told them, echoing the Scriptures, on May 6, 2000, while the Jubilee Year and the Third Millennium were being celebrated:

> you have left father and mother, brothers and sisters, fields and houses, for a spiritual and religious value. In reality, you have committed yourself for a certain time to an important service for the Bishop of Rome and Successor of Peter. You have decided to assure him of the security needed so that he may devote himself freely and without hindrances to men and may announce the Gospel to them.[6]

Epilogue

NAPOLEON BONAPARTE, no mean judge of military and political strength, once remarked that the pope's moral authority was equivalent to "a corps of 200,000 men." Since Wellington was able to defeat Napoleon, the greatest of modern generals, at the battle of Waterloo with a force much smaller than that, the natural power of the popes should be thought of as very high indeed. And Napoleon had not seen the immense growth in the moral stature of the papacy that was to occur during the twentieth and twenty-first centuries. Yet for the past half millennium, the Roman Catholic Church has relied on a tiny body of young Swiss volunteers — rarely over two hundred and usually not much more than half that number — for the essential task of protecting the person of the pope.

As the preceding pages have made clear, during that long service the Swiss Guard has of necessity had to adapt its operations to the particular kind of mission that the various pontiffs have tried to carry out at different moments in history. When the guards were founded in the sixteenth century, popes had to function partly as Renaissance princes and relied heavily on political and economic independence to safeguard the religious mission. The Swiss in those early years had to be real soldiers. They had direct experience of battle, both in the general defense of the Papal States and in the more immediate task of furnishing a corp of papal bodyguards. In those early years, officers and men alike paid dearly with their lives for the honor.

The Swiss Guard weathered many external threats and internal problems over the next five centuries. The guards did not have to confront actual military assaults again after the 1527 sack of

Rome until Napoleon himself came (twice) to carry the pope into exile. The periodic uprisings in the nineteenth century — particularly the revolutionary surges of 1848 and 1870 — and the Nazi occupation of Rome in the 1940s put new military responsibilities in the hands of the Swiss Guard, which they handled better than might have been expected given that they are always outnumbered in terms of sheer manpower when serious political change is under way. The disproportion between the exalted role the Swiss are asked to play and the actual force that they can deploy has called for a skillful combination of military tactics and diplomatic finesse. Anyone looking fairly at the overall record would have to say that they have managed this difficult balancing act very well.

The role of the Guard in recent decades has shifted substantially. Military men have sometimes been heard to deplore how the Swiss have allegedly "fallen" from their original martial status to a merely ceremonial function. This is both unfair and inaccurate. The Swiss do have a ceremonial role at large Vatican celebrations, but they continue to perform essential security services. Indeed, it seems clear that while the Swiss Guard may wear sixteenth-century uniforms for the public appearances of the pope, they are at the same time being drawn into the twenty-first-century struggle to secure the movements of public figures amid a rising tide of terrorism around the globe. One of the great challenges facing the officers and men of the Swiss Guard for some years has been the determination of modern popes to become universal pastors and in the process to come as close as they possibly can to people wherever they go. In modern conditions, there is no need for the Swiss Guard to be a military force. The guards have the much more difficult and delicate task of daily weighing risks and benefits as the pope goes about his pastoral mission.

As the role of the modern papacy has become more purified, so has the role of the Guard. The young Swiss who apply for papal service today know they are not likely to face direct military assaults, though given the state of the world, they will train to a certain extent, if they are accepted by Rome, for those eventualities too. Almost universally, those young men talk about the attraction they felt to a vocation: protecting and possibly having to give up your life for the Holy Father — the same idealism that has drawn Swiss to papal service down through the centuries. Most modern guards will give up two or three years of their lives in their twenties, will suffer some in their immediate finances and careers because of their time in Rome, and may have to delay getting married. They will spend long hours alone on guard duty, especially when they get assigned the tedious jobs of the new recruits, and may not receive much thanks for it except for the occasional words of the pope himself. But anyone who spends time with the modern Swiss guards will see that they do not work for the kinds of day-to-day gratification that most of us expect in a job. They have a vocation, even if it is only for a few years. For all its rigors, it's the kind of service that few of us are lucky enough to get to do. The Swiss guards know this, as do the Swiss, Catholic and Protestant, in Switzerland who take pride in the work. And that is why the tradition of the Papal Swiss Guard has not only survived but shows strong signs of continuing vigor for the twenty-first century and beyond.

Notes

Chapter One / Five Hundred Years of Fortitude

1. See page 158 in this volume.
2. Conversation with the author, Rome, November 3, 2004.
3. Ibid.
4. Personal interview with the author.
5. Quoted in Glauco Benigni, *Gli angeli custodi del Papa* (Turin: UTET Libreria, 2004), 29.
6. Ibid., 35–36.
7. Ibid., 37.

Chapter Two / "Defenders of the Church's Liberty"

1. Douglas Miller and Gerry Embleton, *The Swiss at War, 1300–1500* (Osceola, WI: Osprey, 2004), 31.
2. Preface by Swiss conseiller fédéral Motta in Gaston Castella, *La garde fidèle du Saint-Père: Les soldats suisses au service du Vatican de 1506 à nos jours* (Paris: Aux Editions de la Clé d'Or, 1935), n.p.
3. Quoted in ibid., 21.
4. Niccolò Machiavelli, *The Art of War*, Book VII.
5. On this point, see John McCormack, *One Million Mercenaries: Swiss Soldiers in the Armies of the World* (London: Leo Cooper, 1993).
6. Castella, *La garde fidèle*, 20.
7. For a lively description of the Swiss Army today, see John McPhee, *La place de la concorde suisse* (New York: Farrar & Strauss, 1984).
8. From Pastor's *History of the Popes*, quoted in Castella, *La garde fidèle*, 32.
9. Christine Shaw, *Julius II: The Warrior Pope* (Oxford: Blackwell, 1993), 8.
10. Jacob Burckhardt, *The Civilization of the Renaissance in Italy*, trans. S. G. C. Middlemore (New York: Penguin, 1990), 90.
11. A charming account of this whole period, which corrects many of the misimpressions given wide currency by popular films such as *The Agony and the Ecstasy*, is Ross King's *Michelangelo and the Pope's Ceiling* (New York: Penguin, 2003).

12. Shaw, *Julius II*, 124.
13. Ibid., 101.
14. Ibid., 103.
15. Paul M. Krieg, *Die Schweizergarde in Rom* (Lucerne: Räber-Verlag, 1960), 14–16.
16. Niccolò Machiavelli, *Discourses on Livy,* trans. Harvey C. Mansfield and Nathan Tarcov (Chicago: University of Chicago Press, 1966), 62 (I, 27:1).
17. Shaw, *Julius II,* 156.
18. Quoted from Paolo Giovio in Castella, *La Garde fidèle,* 41.
19. Castella, *La garde fidèle,* 6.
20. Quoted in Shaw, *Julius II,* 313.
21. Quoted in ibid., 351.
22. Burckhardt, *Civilization of the Renaissance,* 148.

Chapter Three / Consolidation and Trial

1. Gaston Castella, *La garde fidèle du Saint-Père: Les soldats suisses au service du Vatican de 1506 à nos jours* (Paris: Aux Editions de la Clé d'Or, 1935), 82.
2. Christopher Hibbert, *Rome: The Biography of a City* (New York: Penguin, 1985), 147.
3. Paul M. Krieg, *Die Schweizergarde in Rom* (Lucerne: Räber-Verlag, 1960).
4. Castella, *La garde fidèle,* 93–94.
5. Ibid., 95.
6. Krieg, *Die Schweizergarde,* 28.
7. Ibid., 34.
8. Ibid., 37.
9. Ibid., 40.
10. Judith Hook, *The Sack of Rome, 1527* (London: Macmillan, 1972), 26–27.
11. Ibid., 97.
12. Ibid., 100.
13. Ibid., 134.
14. Krieg, *Die Schweizergarde,* 44.
15. Quoted in Hook, *Sack of Rome,* 140, from the diaries of Marino Sanuto.
16. Quoted in ibid., 143, from the Sanuto diaries.
17. Ibid., 165.
18. Ibid., 186.

Chapter Four / Siege, Dissolution, Rebirth

1. Augustus J. C. Hare, *Walks in Rome* (New York: Macmillan, 1896), 492.
2. From William Stewart Rose's nineteenth-century translation.
3. See Ludwig Pastor, *History of the Popes, from the Close of the Middle Ages Drawn from the Secret Archives of the Vatican and Other Original Sources,* 40 vols. (St. Louis: Herder, 1923–69), 9:395, 399, 400, 421, 423, for further details.
4. Benvenuto Cellini, *My Life,* trans. Julia Conway Bondanella and Peter Bondanella (New York: Oxford University Press, 2002), 65.
5. Ibid., 62.
6. Quoted in Pastor, *History of the Popes,* 427.
7. Ibid., 445–46.
8. Paul M. Krieg, *Die Schweizergarde in Rom* (Lucerne: Räber-Verlag, 1960), 49.
9. Christopher Hibbert, *Rome: The Biography of a City* (New York: Penguin, 1985), 160.
10. Pastor, *History of the Popes,* 456.
11. Krieg, *Die Schweizergarde,* 52.
12. Ibid., 54–55.
13. On this point, see André Chastel, *The Sack of Rome, 1527,* translated from the French by Beth Archer (Princeton, N.J.: Princeton University Press, 1983), 200ff.
14. Krieg, *Die Schweizergarde,* 56.
15. Ibid., 57.
16. Ibid., 58.
17. Ibid., 59.
18. Ibid., 65.
19. Ibid., 66.
20. Philip Hughes, *A Popular History of the Catholic Church* (New York: Image, 1962), 181.
21. Krieg, *Die Schweizergarde,* 71.

Chapter Five / Years of Peace — and Napoleonic War

1. Gaston Castella, *La garde fidèle du Saint-Père: Les soldats suisses au service du Vatican de 1506 à nos jours* (Paris: Aux Editions de la Clé d'Or, 1935), 129–30.
2. Ibid., 133.
3. Ibid., 141.
4. See above, page 56.
5. Paul M. Krieg, *Die Schweizergarde in Rom* (Lucerne: Räber-Verlag, 1960), 92.

6. Ibid., 96.
7. Ibid., 100.
8. Castella, *La garde fidèle*, 143.
9. Sources disagree on whether these twenty-five were all Swiss guards or were a combination of about a dozen guards and another dozen Swiss then living in Rome and seeking positions in some form of papal service.
10. Krieg, *Die Schweizergarde*, 104, quoting from Segesser's dispatches.
11. Castella, *La garde fidèle*, 147.
12. Ibid., 145–46.
13. Christopher Hibbert, *Rome: The Biography of a City* (New York: Penguin, 1985), 226.
14. Ibid., 228.
15. Ibid., 231.
16. Ibid.
17. Ibid., 235.
18. Castella, *La garde fidèle*, 152.
19. Ibid., 153.

Chapter Six / The Guard during the Unification of Italy and the Pope's Imprisonment in the Vatican

1. Christopher Hibbert, *Rome: The Biography of a City* (New York: Penguin, 1985), 249.
2. Paul M. Krieg, *Die Schweizergarde in Rom* (Lucerne: Räber-Verlag, 1960), 340.
3. E. E. Y. Hales, *Pio Nono* (New York: Image Books, 1962), 98.
4. Monsignor Krieg lists Alexander Pfyffer, Peter Herzog, Kaspar Oberholzer, Martin Grütter, Josef Herzog, and Florin Dercutins (340).
5. Quoted in Krieg, *Die Schweizergarde*, 342.
6. Ibid., 343.
7. David I. Kertzer, *Prisoner of the Vatican: The Pope's Secret Plot to Capture Rome from the New Italian State* (Boston: Houghton Mifflin, 2004), 9. Despite the unnecessarily lurid and biased subtitle (since the popes ruled Rome for almost fifteen hundred years, their interests were hardly a "secret plot"), this book presents a clear history of the papacy during the period of Italian unification.
8. Quoted in Krieg, *Die Schweizergarde*, 302.
9. Ibid., 305.
10. Quoted in Eamon Duffy, *Saints and Sinners: A History of the Popes* (New Haven: Yale University Press, 2001), 262.
11. Denis Mack Smith, *Italy: A Modern History* (Ann Arbor: University of Michigan Press, 1959), offers a good short account of this process.

12. Much of the following narrative is drawn from the introductory material and memoirs of R. d'Argence, an otherwise unknown Frenchman who served in the Papal Zouaves during this period: *Six mois aux Zouaves pontificaux, ou Les dernier jours des états pontificaux 1870*, ed. Dominic M. Pedrazzini (Bâle: Société Suisse des Traditions Populaires en collaboration avec la Bibliothèque Militaire Fédérale à Berne, 2000).

13. Kertzer, *Prisoner of the Vatican*, 85–86.

14. Krieg, *Die Schweizergarde*, 376.

Chapter Seven / The Guard during the Two World Wars and the Nazi Occupation of Rome

1. Anonymous dispatch, *New York Times*, August 3, 1903, 2.

2. Jules Repond, *Le costume de la garde suisse pontificale et la renaissance italienne* (Rome: Polyglotte Vaticane, 1917).

3. *New York Times*, March 25, 1924, 1.

4. See Frank J. Coppa, "Mussolini and the Concordat of 1929," in *Controversial Concordats: The Vatican's Relations with Napoleon, Mussolini, and Hitler*, ed. Frank J. Coppa (Washington: Catholic University of America Press, 1999), 81–119.

5. Ibid., 87.

6. Quoted in ibid., 89.

7. Quoted in Antonio Serrano, *Die Schweizergarde der Päpste* (Dachau: Bayerland, 1996), 113.

8. See Owen Chadwick, *Britain and the Vatican during the Second World War* (New York: Cambridge University Press, 1986), 160, and references.

9. Ibid., 272.

10. *New York Times*, October 9, 1943, 4.

11. "Jane Scrivener" (pseudonym), *Inside Rome with the Germans* (New York: Macmillan Company, 1945), 4.

12. Ibid., 25.

13. Alexander Good, *Errinerungen: Wacht ins Gwehr* [sic], is a series of vignettes that appeared in the magazine of former Swiss guards *Der Exgardist* from 1992 until 2000.

14. Robert Katz, *The Battle for Rome* (New York: Simon & Schuster, 2003), 40.

15. Dan Kurzman, *The Race for Rome* (New York: Doubleday, 1975), 39.

16. Katz, *Battle for Rome*, 193–94.

17. For the best balanced assessment of the various claims, see John Lukacs, "Questions about Pius XII," in *Remembered Past* (Wilmington: ISI Books, 2005), 507–16.

Chapter Eight / The Guard after World War II

1. Glauco Benigni, *Gli angeli custodi del Papa* (Turin: UTET Libreria, 2004), 40.

2. See John Follain, *City of Secrets: The Truth behind the Murders at the Vatican* (New York: William Morrow, 2003). Follain shows no little prejudice against the Vatican and desperately tries to prove some larger motivation. His failure is perhaps the best evidence that there was no secret scandal.

3. Ibid., 24–25.

4. Ibid., 21.

5. Personal interview with the author, June 22, 2005.

6. "Discours du Pape Jean-Paul II à la Garde Suisse à l'occasion du 6 Mai 2000," quoted in Walter Schaufelberger, *Rencontre avec la Garde Suisse Pontificale* (Vatican City State: Tipografia Vaticana, 2000), 5.

Index

Adrian VI, 50, 62–63, 64
Agca, Mehmet Ali, 4, 177, 183–84, 187–88
Alexander VI, 36, 97
Amlehn, Nikolaus, 106
Antoninus Pius, 77
Apostolic Palace, 9, 12, 17–18, 25, 179
Arch of Bells (Carlo Magno, Charlemagne), 8
Arco delle Campane, 8, 165
Ardinghelli (cardinal), 90
Ariosto, 81
Armellini (cardinal), 80
Art of War (Machiavelli), 35
assassination attempts, 176–77
Austria
   dominant in Venice and Lombardy, 144
   Italians' defeat of, 146
   war against, 139–40
Austrian Habsburgs, defense against, 38–39

Babylonian Captivity, 32, 36
Bachmann, Dhani, 6
Bachmann, Frowin, 23
Badoglio, Pietro, 163
Baglioni, Giovampagnolo, 46
Battle of Lepanto, 101, 108–12
Battle of Marignano (1515), 37–38
Battle of Sedan, 145
Baumgartner, Erasmus, 129
Bembo, Pietro, 53
Benedict XIV, 116
Benedict XV, 160
Benedict XVI, 7, 16–18, 179–80, 181
Berthier, Louis-Alexandre, 118
Berweger, Bartleme, 61

bin Laden, Osama, 186
bodyguard services, 181–82
Bonaparte, Elsa, 121
Bonaparte, Joseph, 118, 121
Bonaparte, Letizia, 121
Bonaparte, Lucien, 121
Bonaparte, Napoleon. *See* Napoleon
Boniface IV, 79
Bramante, Donato, 29, 65
Brantôme, Pierre de, 36
Braschi, Giannangelo (Pius VI), 116–17
bribery, 14
Bronze Doors (Portone di Bronzo), 8, 9, 10
Buchs-Bins, Roland, 178–79, 188, 189, 191
Burckhardt, Jacob, 42, 47, 49

Cajetan (cardinal), 83, 98
camerlengo, 11, 16–17
Campagna, 88
campanilismo, 143
Campo de' Fiori, 45
Campus Martius (Field of Mars), 78
Carabinieri, 123
Carafa, Alfonso, 105
Carafa, Carlo, 105
Carpi (count), 51
Casa di Santa Maria, 13, 17
Casaroli, Agostino, 182
Castel Gandolfo, 24, 149
Castel Sant'Angelo, 69, 76, 77–83, 118, 119, 128, 147
Castiglione, Baldassare, 67
Catholic Action, 160
Catholic Church
   concordats of, 159–61
   threats to, in twentieth century, 31–32

Cavour, Camillo, 144, 149
Celik, Oral, 184
Cellini, Benvenuto, 82–83
Centanni, Gerardo, 181
Cerretti, Bonaventura, 160
Cervantes, Miguel de, 110
Charles V, 3, 60, 62, 65–66, 68, 69, 72, 86–87, 89
Charles VII, 43
Charles IX, 107–8
Chesterton, G. K., 111
Chiaramonti, Giorgio Barnaba (Pius VII), 119–21
CIA, 184, 186
Civic guards, replacing Swiss guards during Italian unification, 126
Clark, Mark, 174
Clement VII, 3, 4, 32, 50, 53, 63–76, 85–86, 88–89, 91, 127
Clement XIII, 116
Clement XIV, 115–16
Coco, Pino, 23
Colonna, Marcantonio, 110, 111–12
Colonna, Pompeio, 68–69, 85–86
Colonna family, 66, 68–71, 73
Committees for National Liberation, 173
conciliar movement, 33
Concordat (1929), 159, 161–64
concordats, 159–61
Confederatio Helvetica (*die Eidgenossenschaft*), 39
Congress of Vienna, 128, 129
Constance, Council of, 33
Corpo di Vigilanza dello Stato Vaticano (Security corps of the Vatican State), 22, 181, 184
Cortile of the Belvedere, 174
Cortile San Damaso, 15, 25
Council of Constance, 33
Council of Trent, 97, 101, 102–3
Counter-Reformation, 99, 101

d'Argence, R., 201n.12
de Coligny, Gaspard, 108
De Courten, Louis Martin, 151–53
del Monte, Giovanni Maria (Julius III), 97
del Val, Merry (cardinal), 156–57
de' Medici, Catherine, 107–8
de' Medici, Giovanni, 50, 51. *See* Leo X
de' Medici, Giovanni Angelo. *See* Pius IV
de' Medici, Giulio, 50, 63, 69–70. *See* Clement VII
Die Vereidigung (swearing-in ceremony), 24–28
Duphot, Léon, 118
d'Urbina, Gian, 83

electronic eavesdropping, 14–15, 182–83
Estermann, Alois, 186–89

Faber, Johannes, 56
Farnese, Alessandro. *See* Paul III
Fascist Party, Church's relationship with, 161–62
Feer, Baptist, 104
Ferdinand (king of Spain), 35, 42
Filonardi (cardinal), 90
Fleckenstein, Jost, 114
Fleckenstein, Nikolaus, 114
Florentine, 91
Follain, John, 202n.2
France. *See also* French Revolution
 Church-State relations in, 54–55
 revolt of 1848, 139
 September Treaty with, 146
Francis I, 47, 54, 55
Franco, Girolamo, 90
French Revolution, 116–17, 138
Friday Riot, 73
Fugger family, 45

Galletti, Giuseppe, 123–26
Garde de Cent Suisses, 30
Garibaldi, Giuseppe, 128, 144, 145
Gendarmeria Pontificia (Pontifical police), 22
Giovio, Paolo, 3, 53, 75

Göldli, Herkules, 4, 75, 87
Göldli, Kaspar, 60
Gonzaga, Francesco, 81
Good, Alexander, 168–71, 174
Governatorato, 22, 169–70
Grab, Amédée, 191
Graf, Christopher, 23
Gray Wolves, 177, 184
Gregory the Great, 79
Gregory XIII, 113
Gregory XVI, 125, 135
Guardia Civile Scelta (Select civil guard), 22
Guardia FC, 24
Guicciardini, Francesco, 35, 49, 67, 73

Hadrian, 77, 78
halberds, 8, 19, 27, 37, 39, 150
Hasler, Peter, 23
Henneberg, Wilhelm, 106
Henry VIII, 34–35
Hertenstein family, 57
Hirschbühl, Alois, 158
Hitler, Adolf, 163, 171–72, 173
Holy League, 48, 109, 110
Holy Office Gate, 8
Honor Guard of His Holiness, 21

Il Cortegiano (Castiglione), 67
infallibility, papal, 146–47, 148
Inspectorate of Public Safety, 181
Isabella (queen of Spain), 35, 42
Islam, aggression of, 109
Italian League, 67, 70, 81
Italy
  foreign incursions into, 52–55
  unification movement in, 124–28, 141, 142–47

Jehle, Alois, 23
Jesuits, 101–2
John of Austria, Don, 110
John XXIII, 14–15, 20, 180
John Paul II, 4, 7–8, 10–13, 14, 18, 154, 177–86, 189–90, 192

Julius II, 4, 29–30, 32, 40–49, 52, 64, 97
Julius III, 97

Kanzler, Hermann von, 147, 148
Kapitulation, 129–31
Kelley, Francis C., 160
Knights and Broken Lances, 21
Krohn, Juan Fernandez, 184

Lannoy, 71, 72
Last Judgment (Michelangelo), 91
Lateran Treaty (1929), 145, 158, 161–62
Latour (general), 127
Law of Guarantees, 149, 160
League of Cambrai, 46
Leo X, 50, 51–57, 59–61, 64, 67, 97
Leo XII, 130, 134
Leo XIII, 151, 154, 155
Leonine City, 69, 145, 150, 159
Lepanto, Battle of, 101, 108–12
"Lepanto" (Chesterton), 111
Loriti, Heinrich, 94
L'Osservatore Romano, 167
Louis XI, 30
Louis XII, 53–54
Louis XVI, 36
Ludovico il Moro, 45

Machiavelli, 35, 46, 52, 53
Mäder, Elmar Theodor, 6, 7–8, 10–11, 16–17, 23, 189–90, 192
Marazzani (monsignor), 133
Marcellus II, 97
Marcus Aurelius, 77
Marignano, Battle of (1515), 37–38, 54, 55
Martin V, 33
Maximilian, 34
McLaughlin, Richard John, 185
Medici family, 50, 52, 68, 73. *See also* de' Medici listings.
Medici, Ferdinand I, 113
Meier, Anna-Lina, 187

Mendoza, Benjamin, 177
mercenaries
  renewed Swiss opposition to, 45
  rise of, 38–40
  Swiss units, 36–37, 43–44
Meyer von Schauensee, Franz Xaver Leopold, 123, 125–28, 136–42, 151, 191
MI-6, 184
Michelangelo, 4, 29–30, 42, 49, 65, 91
Milizia Urbana del Popolo di Roma (Urban Militia of the Roman people), 21–22
Moncada, Ugo, 70
Montelupo, Raffaello da, 81
Montini, Giovanni Battista (Paul VI), 182
Moro, Ludovico il, 45
Muslims, tensions with Western Europe, 56–57
Mussolini, Benito, 158–59, 160–63
Myconius, Oswald, 94

Napoleon, 117–18, 120–21, 138, 159–60, 193, 194
Napoleon III, 145
Napoleonic War, 117–20
Nazis, treatment of Vatican, 166–67
Nicholas V, 80
Noble Guards, 21
Nölly, Hanns, 111
Nünlist, Robert, 175

Operation Old Friend, 186
Opus Dei, 188
Orlando, Vittorio Emmanuele, 160
Orsini family, 68
Oudinot, Charles, 128
Our Lady of Victory, Feast of, 109

Palatine Guards, 21–22, 155
Palazzo della Cancelleria, 122
Palazzo della Signoria (Florence), 73
Palma (bishop), 123

papacy
  changes in, during twentieth century, 154–55
  foreign concern for, during Italian unification, 127
  gaining in stature after abolition of Papal States, 143
  independence of, 33–34
  loss of direct political power, 121
  military role of, 46–47
  modern, threats facing, 176
  purification of, in modern times, 194–95
  in sixteenth-century Europe, 30
  threats to, as spiritual entity, 34–35
  weakened state of, before Julius II, 32–35
papal conclaves, 10–11, 13–18, 104–5, 155, 157, 158, 183
papal infallibility, 146–47, 148
papal residence, 179
Papal States, 33–34, 41–42
  abolition of, 138, 143–47
  changes in (late 1840s), 122
  end of, 142–47
  Julius II's retaking Bologna for, 46
  Napoleon's occupation of, 118
  Swiss Guard fighting for, 140
  troops for, 138
Papal Zouaves, 145, 157
Partito Popolare, 161
Pasanisi, Francesco, 183
Passetto, 3
Pastor, Ludwig, 40, 86, 88
Paul III, 63, 90, 91–92, 96
Paul IV, 97–98, 101
Paul VI, 7, 20–21, 22, 176–77, 180, 182
Perugia, role of, in early Swiss Guard history, 46
Peter, St., 78
Pfyffer, Jost, 106
Pfyffer von Altishofen, Franz, 177
Pfyffer von Altishofen, Franz Ludwig, 115

Index

Pfyffer von Altishofen, Heinrich, 164, 167, 175
Pfyffer von Altishofen, Ignaz, 132–33
Pfyffer von Altishofen, Johann Konrad, 115
Pfyffer von Altishofen, Johann Rudolf, 114
Pfyffer von Altishofen, Karl, 120–21
Pfyffer von Altishofen, Karl Leodegar, 128–35
Pfyffer von Altishofen, Ludwig, 119, 132
Pfyffer von Altishofen, Martin, 129, 132–36
Pfyffer von Altishofen family, 114
Piazza San Bernardino, 151
Pitteloud, Jean Daniel, 23
Pius IV, 102–3, 105–6
Pius V, 103, 106, 107, 109–10, 113
Pius VI (Giannangelo Braschi), 116–17, 119, 159
Pius VII (Giorgio Barnaba Chiaramonti), 119–21, 129, 160
Pius IX, 23, 122, 124–25, 127, 129, 136, 140–42, 151, 145–50
Pius VIII, 134
Pius X, 155–57
Pius XI, 153, 158, 159, 160–61
Pius XII, 14–15, 21, 164, 167–68, 173, 174, 182
Ponte degli Angeli, 77
Pontificia Helvetiorum Cohors. See Swiss Guard
Ponzetti (cardinal), 83
popes
  behaving like secular rulers, 40–41
  contemporary threats to, 180–86
  influence of, 14
  kidnapping, 171–72
  as prisoner of the Vatican, 145, 147, 149–50, 154
  as ruler of earthly and spiritual realm, 144
Porta del Popolo, 45, 73
Porta Santo Spirito, 69

Portone di Bronzo, 25, 158, 165
Pucci, Antonio, 60

Quanta Cura (Pius IX), 146
Quirinale Palace, 123, 135, 150

Radet, Etienne, 120
Raphael, 5, 65
Ratzinger, Joseph, 16, 18. *See also* Benedict XVI
Reagan, Ronald, 178
Red Brigades, 176
Reformation, early politics during, 62–63
Reislauf, 37
Repond, Jules, 155–58
Riedi, Marcel, 187
Röist, Diethelm, 58
Röist, Kaspar, 3–4, 58–63, 71–72, 75, 158
Röist, Marx (Marcus), 57–58
Romano, Giulio, 65
Roman Question, 160, 162
Rome
  capture of, in movement toward Italian unification, 145
  liberation of, 172–74
  occupied by German forces, 163–68
  role of, in Europe, 64–65
  sack of (1527), 3, 50, 74–92, 193–94
Romero, Gladys Meza, 187
Rosin, Albert, 90
Rossi, Pellegrino, 122–23
Rovere, Francesco Maria della, 56
Rovere, Giuliano della, 41. *See also* Julius II
Rudolph (Holy Roman Emperor), 39
Rueckers, Adolfo, 175
Rusconi, Giovanni, 135–36

sack of the Colonna (*Sacco dei Colonna*), 69
Sacro Possesso, 51–52
Sala Clementina, 24
sala di pianto, 16
Samet, Aslan, 184

San Sebastiano, Church of, 112
Sandinistas, 185
Sant'Anna Gate, 8, 176
Santo Spirito, 75
Sapienza University, 65
Sarto, Giuseppe Melchiorre. *See* Pius X
Schiner, Matthew, 47–49, 50–51, 55
Sedan, Battle of, 145
Segesser, Albrecht, 103, 107
Segesser, Jost, 103, 106–8, 110–13
Segesser, Stephan-Alexander, 113–14
Segmüller, Pius, 189–90
Sendero Luminoso, 184
September Treaty, 146
Serbelloni, Gabriele, 105–6
Sergeant Barbetta, 19
Sforza, Francesco, 66–67
SISMI (Servizi Informazioni Segreto Militare Italiano), 183
Sisters of Divine Providence, 19
Sistine Chapel, 13, 42, 84
Sixtus IV (Francesco della Rovere), 36, 41
Sixtus X, 113
Sodano, Angelo (cardinal), 17, 189
Somalo, Eduardo Martínez, 11, 16–17
Sonderbundskrieg, 142
Sonnenberg, Albert von, 142–43, 147, 148, 151
spies, 14. *See also* electronic eavesdropping
St. John Lateran (basilica), 149
St. Peter's Basilica, 12, 25, 29, 64–65, 77, 84, 176
St. Peter's Square, 10–11, 173, 183–84
Stasi, 188
Sterbini, Pietro, 124, 125
surveillance, of Vatican, 14–15, 182–83
Swiss forces
   mercenary units among, 36–37
   mode of fighting, 37–38
   organized for defense, 38
Swiss Guard
   actions during time of Italian unification, 123–27
   becoming member of, 18–20

Swiss Guard (*continued*)
   behavior of, 8–9
   celebrating four hundredth anniversary, 158
   changing nature of, 191–92, 194
   changing use of, under Leo X, 59–61
   command structure of, 23
   conditions for, after *Kapitulation*, 130–34
   constraints on, 7
   created by Julius XII, 30
   decline of military discipline in, 150–51
   defending Rome against Colonna, 69
   disbanding of, after sack of Rome, 87–89
   divided into watches, 96
   facing competition for members against Naples, 131
   fighting for the Papal States, 140
   final responsibility for pope's safety, 4
   finances for members, 5–6, 90, 93, 96, 114, 130, 131, 136, 140–42, 151, 175
   financial challenges under Clement VII, 68
   first non-white member, 6
   first recruits, 44–47
   firsthand account from World War II, 168–71
   honored for role during uprisings (mid-1800s), 141–42
   improved status under Paul IV, 98
   in Jubilee Years, 64, 190
   keeping the peace during World War II, 168
   in late nineteenth century, 151–53
   legal status of, in Vatican, 22–24
   Leo X claiming, for personal rather than military assistance, 52
   marital regulations, 115, 131, 137
   military discipline restored for, 141
   modern responsibilities of, 7
   new military responsibilities of, 194
   opposition to Axis powers, 164

Swiss Guard (*continued*)
  order established among, under Jost Segesser, 107
  origins of, 29–49
  outbreak within (October 1827), 132–34
  participation in naval battle of Lepanto, 108–12
  penury and squalid living conditions for, 135–36
  postwar calm for, 175
  Protestants desiring entry, 191
  protocols for special visitors, 23
  purification of, in modern times, 194–95
  quiet period (1592–1790s), 112–16
  reaction against military training, 155–57
  recalled (1527), 71–72
  reconstituted under Meyer, 128
  reconstituting, after sack of Rome, 90–94
  recruiting, 5, 6, 18–20, 24, 30, 92–93, 95, 96, 127–28, 137, 150, 178, 190–91
  reform of regulations for, under Meyer, 137–38
  renewed confidence in, 158–59
  requirements for joining, 5–6
  restored after French Revolution, 120–21
  retaking Milan from the French, 53
  return to military discipline among, 115
  Röist's reform of, 57–59
  role during assault against Rome (1867–70), 147–51
  roles for, in early twentieth century, 155
  during sack of Rome (1527), 74–75, 80, 82, 193–94
  security functions of, 9–10
  shift to ceremonial role, 114–15
  spiritual formation of members, 6
  staffing of, 23–24
  stationed in Italian cities, 102

Swiss Guard (*continued*)
  status of, 1815–49, 128–42
  studies of, ix
  supporting military and political aims of Julius II, 47–49
  swearing-in ceremony, 24–28
  training of, 19–20, 179
  under direct control of the pope, 22–23
  uniforms of, 4–5, 19, 20, 131, 158
  weapons of, 7–8, 147, 150, 179
Switzerland. *See also* Swiss forces
  ban on foreign military service, 62
  desiring permanent representative in Roman Curia, 99
  early Swiss service to the pope, 35–36
  formalized relations with Holy See, 112–13
  Holy See's goals for (late sixteenth century), 101–2
  neutrality of, 44, 56, 129
  occupied by Napoleonic forces, 119
  papal politics and, 47–49
  renewed spirit in, after sack of Rome, 92–94
  renewed Swiss commitment to the pope, 56–57
  reputation of Swiss as fighting force, 35, 44
  requesting return of some Swiss guards for active duty during World War I, 157
  response to perceived Turkish threat, 108
  silence in, about the sack of Rome, 89–90
  as source of infantry for France, 55–56
Swiss Federal Council, after Concordat of 1929, 162
Swiss mentality, 6
Swiss military tactics, 39–40
Syllabus of Errors, 146

terrorism, response to, 8
Theatines, 98

Tornay, Cédric, 187–89
Trastevere, 61, 62, 69, 148
Treaty of Westphalia, 112, 114
Trent, Council of, 97, 101, 102–3
Turks, threat of, 90, 98, 101 105, 107, 108–12

Urban VI, 32

Vasari, Giorgio, 54
Vatican. *See also individual listings for buildings and places*
   bombed during World War II, 169–71
   entrances manned by Swiss Guard, 8
   improvements under Clement VII's papacy, 64–65
   limiting public presence during World War II, 165
   modernization of, 159
   modern terrorist threats against, 175–76
   Museum, 42
   political neutrality of, 161–62
   reemerging as political entity during World War II, 164
   relationship with Italy, 145
Vatican Council I, 146
Vatican Council II, 175–76
Venturi, Pietro Tacchi, 161

Vergés, Jacques, 189
Via delle Fornaci, 75
Via Rasella, 173
Victor Emmanuel, 143, 145, 149, 150
Villot, Jean, 21
Vittorio Emmanuele III, 163
Volpe (cardinal), 106
von Beroldingen, Josue, 91
von Hertenstein, Peter, 44–45, 57
von Meggen, Jost, 92–100, 103
von Meggen, Nikolaus, 91–92
von Silenen, Christoph, 57, 59
von Silenen, Kaspar, 44–45, 56, 57
von Silenen, Kaspar Leo, 103–5
von Weizsäcker, Ernst, 172
Waldstätte (Forest Cantons), 38
Wars of Religion, 112
Wiesenmeyer, Heiny, 94–95
Wojtyla, Karol, 18, 182–83. *See also* John Paul II
Wolff, Karl, 172
World War I, 157–62
World War II, 163–74

Yousef, Ramzi Ahmed, 185

Zumbrunnen, Hans, 102
Zwingli, Huldrych, 48, 55, 62

Of Related Interest

Robert Royal
CATHOLIC MARTYRS OF THE TWENTIETH CENTURY
A Comprehensive World History

If you think martyrdom happened only to early Christians in Rome, think again! Royal shows how Christian martyrdom is more common today than ever before. He presents the first comprehensive history of the twentieth-century martyrs. This volume traces specific situations all over the world, recounts how martyrdoms occurred, studies the political systems, and offers a rich collection of individual biographies.

0-8245-1846-2, hardcover

Robert Royal
DANTE ALIGHIERI
Divine Comedy, Divine Spirituality

A popular presentation of the spiritual genius of Dante, as revealed in his great epic *The Divine Comedy,* a literary classic that is enjoying a renaissance as a spiritual masterpiece as well.

978-0-8245-2414-2, paperback

crossroad

Of Related Interest

H. J. Fischer, Veteran Vatican Journalist
POPE BENEDICT XVI
A Personal Portrait

Inspired by the author's thirty-year personal and professional relationship with Joseph Ratzinger.

Dr. Fischer is the ideal biographer of the new Pope. As a theologically trained journalist, a friend of Joseph Ratzinger, and a twenty-five-year Vatican correspondent for Germany's leading daily newspaper, Dr. Fischer has observed and accompanied the professor and cardinal for three decades. He understands the life and work of this gifted church leader as well as the challenges and questions that confront Benedict XVI in his new role.

Includes more than sixty color and black-and-white photos.

978-0-8245-2372-5, hardcover

Support your local bookstore or order directly from the publisher at www.CrossroadPublishing.com

To request a catalog or inquire about quantity orders, please e-mail sales@CrossroadPublishing.com

www.ingramcontent.com/pod-product-compliance
Lightning Source LLC
Chambersburg PA
CBHW040309170426
43195CB00020B/2905